SWIFT

GULLIVER'S TRAVELS

NOTES

COLES EDITORIAL BOARD

Bound to stay open

Publisher's Note

Otabind (Ota-bind). This book has been bound using the patented Otabind process. You can open this book at any page, gently run your finger down the spine, and the pages will lie flat.

ABOUT COLES NOTES

COLES NOTES have been an indispensible aid to students on five continents since 1948.

COLES NOTES are available for a wide range of individual literary works. Clear, concise explanations and insights are provided along with interesting interpretations and evaluations.

Proper use of COLES NOTES will allow the student to pay greater attention to lectures and spend less time taking notes. This will result in a broader understanding of the work being studied and will free the student for increased participation in discussions.

COLES NOTES are an invaluable aid for review and exam preparation as well as an invitation to explore different interpretive paths.

COLES NOTES are written by experts in their fields. It should be noted that any literary judgement expressed herein is just that – the judgement of one school of thought. Interpretations that diverge from, or totally disagree with any criticism may be equally valid.

COLES NOTES are designed to supplement the text and are not intended as a substitute for reading the text itself. Use of the NOTES will serve not only to clarify the work being studied, but should enhance the readers enjoyment of the topic.

ISBN 0-7740-3308-8

© COPYRIGHT 1999 AND PUBLISHED BY
COLES PUBLISHING COMPANY
TORONTO - CANADA
PRINTED IN CANADA

Manufactured by Webcom Limited
Cover finish: Webcom's Exclusive **DURACOAT**

CONTENTS

Jonathan Swift
Life and Works

Biographical Sketch

Though born in Ireland, Jonathan Swift (1667-1745) refused to identify himself with the "savage old Irish," and considered himself an Englishman who had been accidentally "dropped" in Ireland. His ancestors on both sides had been English, and he went to England at the age of 21 when the "native Irish" took up arms in 1688 for King James II, the deposed Roman Catholic monarch of England, Ireland and Scotland.

In England, he became the secretary of Sir William Temple, an important statesman and writer, and a man whom Swift soon grew to greatly admire. "I never read his writings," Swift wrote, "but I prefer him to all others at present in England, which I suppose is all but a piece of self-love." Service with Sir William Temple, continued during the 1690's with interruptions for several returns to Ireland, made Swift acquainted with a number of important people, including even the king, William III. Swift learned much about politics and began to share the literary and intellectual excitement of the times. He attempted poetry, mostly in an elaborate form called the Pindaric ode, but with little success. The story goes that he forever resented the judgment on his poems given by his cousin, John Dryden, the leading English poet of the day: "Cousin Swift, you will never be a poet." After this discouragement Swift never again attempted "flights" in poetry. His future poems would be plain, unadorned, with no effort made to achieve artificial polish or intense emotion. In 1696-7 he wrote, in prose, *The Battle of the Books*, an amusing satire putting Swift on the side of Sir William Temple in a famous literary quarrel about the relative merits of ancient and modern writers.

Meanwhile, Swift had, by special arrangement, received his M.A. degree from Oxford (1692), hoping that the degree might help him to advance in the established English Church. But, receiving no church favors in England, he returned to Ireland, was ordained an Anglican priest (1695) and began his clerical ministry at Kilroot. May of 1696 found him back at Temple's estate, Moor Park, where he remained until, as Swift put it, "all that was good and amiable among men" died with Sir William in 1699. Swift was soon back in Ireland as secretary and chaplain to the Earl of Berkeley in Dublin Castle. But Sir William had left behind a duty for Swift, that of helping to edit for publication his letters and memoirs.

Swift's association with Temple was important in the development of his powers and personality. He met socially cultivated and enlightened people like Temple, Lady Temple and the Earl of Halifax.

1

Temple's well-stocked library, of which Swift took full advantage, was in itself an education. As secretary, Swift not only met important people like the king, but was, in addition, Temple's envoy to discuss even constitutional issues with the king and his adviser, the Earl of Portland. Swift's contact with Temple and with Temple's writings — diplomacy, essays, correspondence — acquainted him with perceptive ideas on history, politics and cultural subjects. He became the tutor of Esther (Hester) Johnson, an intelligent girl of eight who lived in Temple's household. With Esther Johnson, whom he later called "Stella," Swift continued a close friendship until her death in 1728. So close was their friendship that there has always been an unresolved question as to whether the two were married in 1716. They probably were not. Swift and Stella are reported to have never met without having a third person present, though at Swift's urging she settled permanently near him in Ireland, bringing with her an older companion, Rebecca Dingley. Some of Swift's most delightful letters are addressed to these two ladies.

Swift's literary gifts began to attract notice. In 1704, he published in London *A Tale of a Tub* and *The Battle of the Books*, both written some years before. Although published anonymously, their writer was soon generally known among literary men in England, who thus became aware of a new, fully developed and powerful prose satirist in their midst. He had frequent opportunities to be among these men, for he repeatedly visited England between 1700 and 1709. One stay in England (1707-09) lasted 21 months, when he was sent to negotiate with the English government for certain financial advantages for the Established Church of Ireland. When the Whig government gave him no satisfaction in his demands, Swift, more a church man than a party man, switched to support of the Tories, who were about to come into power and who promised the favor he sought. During this stay in London he also greatly amused the town by writing under the pen-name of Isaac Bickerstaff. He started an uproar of merriment with a hoax, in which he insisted and continued to insist that the well-known astrologer, John Partridge, was dead — while Partridge squalled, squirmed, and swore that he was still alive.

Swift remembered 1710-1714 as his years of glory. He was in London all that time. The Tory government flattered and pampered him, and used his incomparable journalistic pen to further their policies. For a time he edited the government's party newspaper, the Tory *Examiner*. He was on the friendliest terms with the two principal ministers of Her Majesty's government, Robert Harley (soon to become the Earl of Oxford) and Henry St. John (soon to be made Viscount Bolingbroke).

From London in those years, he sent to Ireland an almost daily account of his activities and those of London in charming letters to

Stella and "Dingley." Although later published as *Journal to Stella*, the letters were addressed to both ladies.

During these years in London, Swift's wit, geniality, and capacity for friendship made him very much in demand for both glittering occasions and intimate parties. He enjoyed the friendship of leading writers like Alexander Pope and John Gay. A young heiress, Esther Vanhomrigh (Swift called her "Vanessa"), fell desperately in love with him. Swift failed to return her love. Nevertheless, she moved to Ireland to live near him, and the unhappiness of her passion for him ended in scandal and her death in 1723.

Even in those years of glory, however, Swift suffered grievously from attacks of pain and illness resulting from Ménière's disease, which brought him torments of deafness, giddiness, headache and nausea. Swift was often troubled by these attacks, and they may have contributed to the insanity which overtook him in his old age.

Swift also made enemies with his pen. When the question of a reward for his services arose, his attacks on people of influence like the Duke and Duchess of Marlborough and the Duchess of Somerset greatly harmed him. He had hoped for at least a deanship of a church somewhere in England, but he received the position of Dean of St. Patrick's Cathedral in Dublin. His enemies, he thought, had reminded the Queen that he was the author of *A Tale of a Tub*, a book the Queen viewed as wicked. Disappointed and bitter, he went to Ireland — to him, this represented banishment and exile. For six years after Queen Anne's death and the fall of the Tory government, he tended his duties at St. Patrick's, nursed his anger and grumbled (wittily, as always). In England, the triumphant Whigs scattered Swift's friends — to prison, to France and to places of refuge from Whig prosecution.

The 1720's brought Swift's career its greatest triumphs. By championing Irish causes against England in such powerful satiric writings as *The Drapier's Letters* and *A Modest Proposal*, he established himself as the only Irish patriot of the century to unite the Irish effectively. His popularity was solid and immense, so solid that once, when the Whig first minister of England, Robert Walpole, was on the point of arresting Swift, he was advised to send an army of 10,000 men to accomplish the task unless he wished his agents to be torn apart in the Dublin streets. In 1726, the greatest of Swift's writings appeared, *Gulliver's Travels*. He had been at work on it for more than five years, though other works had also been produced in that very busy period.

1726 and 1727, although they brought him the joy of revisiting his old literary friends in England, were overshadowed by the knowledge that Stella was in such ill health that she could not live long. Her death in 1728 ended thirty-five years of perfect friendship. Swift's grief moved him to declare that "there is not a greater folly than to contract too great

3

and intimate a friendship, which must always leave the survivor miserable;" and he asserted that "violent friendship is much more lasting, and as much engaging, as violent love." For his departed friend he wrote "A Prayer for Stella" and the poem "On the Death of Mrs. Johnson."

There still remained much to do. Swift had achieved a place of highest eminence in Ireland in the church, patriotic leadership and in literature. He continued his scrupulous care of St. Patrick's Cathedral, fought all bishops whenever they gave signs of encroaching upon the welfare of the lesser clergy, issued pamphlets aimed at improving Ireland's condition and wrote many of his best poems. All of Dublin celebrated his seventieth birthday.

But then Swift entered into a serious decline. Some three months before he turned seventy-five he was legally declared of unsound mind, unable to care for himself. His last years were pitiful. He had, in his own words, become "a drivel and a show," and after much suffering he died on October 19, 1745. Dublin buried him beside Stella in St. Patrick's Cathedral.

Chronology of Important Dates

1667 —Jonathan Swift born in Dublin, Ireland, November 30.

1686 —Swift at Trinity College, Dublin.

1689 —Swift became secretary in the household of Sir William Temple in Surrey, England. Met "Stella."

1690 —Swift returned to Ireland.

1691 —Swift rejoins Temple household.

1692 —M.A., Oxford. First published poem "Ode to the Athenian Society."

1695 —Ordained as priest in the Church of Ireland (the Irish branch of the Anglican Church).

1699 —With Sir William Temple again; probable date of composition of *A Tale of a Tub.*

1701 —Awarded D.D. (Doctor of Divinity) degree from Dublin University.

1704 —*A Tale of a Tub, The Battle of the Books,* and *The Mechanical Operation of the Spirit* published anonymously.

1707 —Swift in London as emissary of the Irish clergy.

1708 —*The Partridge-Bickerstaff Papers.*

1710 —Swift renounced Whigs, joined Tories; editor of the *Examiner,* a Tory newspaper; began the *Journal to Stella* (September 1, 1710-June 6, 1713).

1711 —*Argument Against Abolishing Christianity; The Conduct of the Allies; Miscellanies in Prose and Verse; A New Journey to Paris.*

1713 —Swift appointed Dean of St. Patrick's Cathedral, Dublin.

1714 —Formation of the Scriblerus Club; beginning of long Whig supremacy under Walpole.

1720 —*A Proposal for the Universal Use of Irish Manufacture*; probable beginning of composition of *Gulliver's Travels*.

1725 —*The Drapier's Letters*; great popularity in Ireland; the British repeal the law which prompted *The Drapier's Letters*.

1726 —Visit to England, as Alexander Pope's house-guest; *Gulliver's Travels* published anonymously.

1727 —Last trip to England; Pope-Swift *Miscellanies*, Vols. I and II published.

1728 —Death of Stella; Pope-Swift *Miscellanies*, Vol. III.

1729 —*A Modest Proposal*.

1732 —Pope-Swift *Miscellanies*, Vol. IV.

1736 —Pope-Swift *Miscellanies*, Vol. V.

1742 —Guardians appointed to care for Swift's affairs, because of mental deterioration.

1745 —Swift died, October 19.

Swift's England

The eighteenth century has been described in many ways. It was called, for example, the "Neoclassic Age," "the Augustan Age," and "The Enlightenment." Perhaps the most common term of designation for this era was the "Age of Reason."

In theory, at least, the eighteenth century was devoted to reason and common sense, literary rules and regulations, and to the spirit of liberty and skepticism. Political and literary historians have, however, discovered wide diversity in this period, and it is misleading to think of this era in terms of convenient labels. The most workable literary arrangement is to divide the period into two parts: Neoclassic and pre-Romantic. The Neoclassic emphasis on the classics and reason held its strongest position in the world of literature in the latter part of the seventeenth century and in the first part of the eighteenth century. In this period, much attention was given to the so-called literary rules for writing. These rules had presumably been derived from such classical writers as Homer, Aristotle and Horace, as well as from more recent Neoclassical critics and authors, such as the French authority, Boileau. The pre-Romantic era, which occurred in the latter part of the eighteenth century, was to lead to the nineteenth-century Romantic Age of Wordsworth, Coleridge, Byron, Shelley and Keats. Pre-Romantic writers placed more emphasis on descriptions of nature, subjective flights of imagination and a wider variety of verse form and meter. Here again, however, it is not very helpful to generalize. Necessary distinctions and exceptions should always be kept in mind.

The Augustan Age in England was characterized by an increasing amount of wealth garnered from trade and manufacturing. At the same time, the condition of the very poor remained unchanged, and people in many parts of Ireland and England were destitute.

The eighteenth century saw a vast increase in reading. Newspapers, magazines and journals of various types were eagerly received. The most famous journal was, of course, *The Spectator*, edited by Richard Steele and Joseph Addison. Men of fashion gathered at the coffee houses, which were extremely popular. At these coffee houses one could gossip, read, discuss literature, politics, science and other topics of the day.

Literature flourished during this period. Not only were *The Spectator* essays popular, but the poetry of Alexander Pope and the work of Daniel Defoe, whose *Robinson Crusoe* was published in 1719, were well received. Swift's *Gulliver's Travels* was, of course, one of the high points among the literary works produced in the early part of the century.

An English group for the advancement of science had been incorporated in 1662, with Robert Boyle as its principal figure. This group was the famous Royal Society. The most important scientist of the Royal

Society during Swift's time was Sir Isaac Newton, who discovered the law of gravitation. Experiments of all kinds were carried on, and science grew in importance. Swift and many of the other men of letters at this time, however, constantly attacked and satirized the Royal Society. Swift and other literati were opposed to pedantry, which they believed the Royal Society fostered. But, most of all, they felt that many scientists were engaged in impractical, far-fetched experiments and theorizing.

One of the most newsworthy events of the time, which also finds mention in *Gulliver's Travels*, was the South Sea Bubble. A South Sea Company was formed during the reign of Queen Anne. This company was designed to develop trade with the Spanish American colonies. Private creditors were persuaded to surrender claims of debt against the government in exchange for share-buying in the company. It was thought that the profits of the South Sea Company would be considerable. Hence, not only government creditors but also private individuals purchased a vast amount of stock. Similar stock companies grew up, and all kinds of wild, impractical get-rich-quick schemes were advertised. Eventually, stock prices rose to incredible heights and a "crash" occurred: the South Sea Bubble broke, and many people lost vast amounts of money.

In philosophical thought, the eighteenth century is usually associated with a belief in reason and nature (although these words had various meanings), skepticism in matters of religion, a belief in progress, and an emphasis on information gathered from the senses and through experiment (scientific empiricism). The Old and New Testaments and the creeds of individual churches were challenged and often rejected, and many eighteenth-century figures adopted a belief in Deism. Deism had different aspects and different characteristics. Its meaning often varied from individual to individual. But, in general, Deism presupposed a belief in God. God was considered to have created the world and to have left it alone. The Deist usually assumed the existence of God by accepting God's handiwork in the beauty of nature and in the marvelous working of the universe. To this belief in God the Deist usually added such ideas as optimism ("Whatever is, is right"), benevolence and toleration of the beliefs of others. Often, the Deist became politically active in advocating freedom and democratic goals.

Historical and Political Background

In order to understand more completely Swift's life, ideas and writings, certain historical and political aspects of the late seventeenth century and early eighteenth century should be known.

In 1688, James II of the House of Stuart was overthrown as king of England. He was succeeded by his daughter, Mary, and by his son-in-law, William of Orange (William III). James II fled to France, and England was ruled by William and Mary. Many of the British, however, still regarded James II as the legitimate king. The people who supported James II were called Jacobites. France sided with James II, and several battles were fought between William's forces and the supporters of James. The English were able to shatter James' hopes by two particularly overwhelming victories — the Battle of the Boyne in Ireland and the naval Battle of La Hogue near the coast of France.

Queen Mary died in 1694, and William III ruled England alone until his death in 1702, when he was succeeded by his wife's sister, Anne. James II died in France in 1701, and the French king recognized James' son, James Edward, as the legitimate king of England.

When the king of Spain died, he willed his throne to the grandson of King Louis XIV of France. Since this combination of Spanish and French power was detrimental to English interests, the English joined forces with Holland, Denmark, Austria and Sweden and fought against the French. Thus began the War of the Spanish Succession (called Queen Anne's War, in America).

The most important military figure in this war was General John Churchill, later Duke of Marlborough. In 1704, Marlborough won a crushing victory over the French at the Battle of Blenheim, a town on the Danube. Marlborough was given considerable money and a large estate by the grateful British, but the War of the Spanish Succession continued to drag on.

The two English political parties — the Whigs and the Tories — grew more powerful. The Whigs were, in general, the Low Church group. They believed that the power of parliament should be increased and that the power of the monarch should be lessened. The Tories, or High Church party, believed in the episcopal rights of the Anglican Church and supported a strong monarchy.

In 1710, a Tory ministry came into power. The Tories desired to end the War of the Spanish Succession, but Marlborough and the other Whigs maintained that the war should be pursued and that the French could be thoroughly defeated. In 1713, the Tory ministry concluded the Treaty of Utrecht with France. This ended the war, but the Whigs were opposed to this treaty since they believed that the peace terms with France were too lenient.

In 1714, Queen Anne died. Because her husband and children had died before her, she was succeeded according to the provisions of the Act of Settlement (1701). This law provided that if Anne died childless, the English throne would be turned over to the Electress Sophia of Hanover and her heirs. Hanover was a small German province. This act was designed to secure a Protestant succession. James II and his sons, the "Pretenders," were Catholics. Since the Electress Sophia had died, her son followed Anne to the throne and became George I of England.

George I immediately preferred the Whigs, and the Tories lost control of the government. George I was fifty-four years old when he became king of England. He did not speak English, and he was inclined to let the Whig party rule the country more or less as it wished. Eventually, Robert Walpole was to become the most important Whig minister. Walpole was an astute politician who knew how to keep his party in control of the government. Political corruption was rampant, and the Tories, who had been accused of Jacobite activities, were excluded from office and patronage. Consequently, the Tories were most critical of the Whig regime. The Tories hoped that George's son, the Prince of Wales, who showed some sympathy for their views, would soon succeed his father and return them to power. When, however, George I died in 1727 and was succeeded by his son, the son (George II) did not justify Tory hopes, but continued to keep the Whigs in power.

There were continuous Jacobite intrigues. Battles between the British and the Jacobite sympathizers took place both in Scotland and in England. The Whigs constantly charged the Tories with treasonable activities and Jacobite tendencies. They attempted to bring both Robert Harley, first earl of Oxford, and Henry St. John, Viscount Bolingbroke, the former Tory ministers, to trial. But Bolingbroke fled to France and, though imprisoned for a time, Oxford was eventually released. In 1722, the Anglican bishop of Rochester, Bishop Atterbury, was accused of being in correspondence with the "Pretender." Atterbury's letters were seized and, it was on the basis of these letters, interpreted by the Whigs, that Atterbury was convicted and banished.

Many of these historical and political elements intimately involve Jonathan Swift and his work. Swift supported the Tory ministry which came to power in 1710. He was very critical of the Whigs for their mistreatment of the Tories and for their political corruption. Parts of *Gulliver's Travels* can, in one sense, be seen as a defence of the conduct of the Tories at a time in which they were politically unpopular.

Introduction to *Gulliver's Travels*

The Origin and Text of the Novel

About 1714, the Scriblerus Club was formed with Alexander Pope, John Arbuthnot, John Gay, Thomas Parnell and Swift as its best-known members. This group published a collection of writings called the *Memoirs of Martinus Scriblerus*, which were intended to satirize pedantry, and "false tastes in learning." As part of the Scriblerus material, Swift chose to write of Martinus' adventures in distant places.

Scriblerus was to travel to a place where he would encounter little people, and he would also travel to a country composed of philosophers. The Scriblerus Club, however, soon disbanded, and Swift apparently put these writings aside until 1720 or 1721 when he began *Gulliver's Travels* in earnest. He probably used some of this early Scriblerus material in the "Voyage to Lilliput" and in the "Voyage to Laputa," but *Gulliver's Travels* in its final form was substantially a new work filled with many political allusions referring to events which occurred after 1714.

Parts I and II were probably written first, and then Swift completed the "Voyage to the Country of the Houyhnhnms" about 1723. By 1725, the *Travels* were completed and revised. Swift wrote to his friend, Charles Ford, on August 14, 1725: "I have finished my Travells, and I am now transcribing them; they are admirable things and will wonderfully mend the World."

In 1726, Swift went to England and, on October 28, 1726, *Gulliver's Travels* was published anonymously by Benjamin Motte. Motte, however, made several printing errors and also made additional omissions in the text. Certain corrections were made by Motte in an edition of the *Travels* which he published in 1727, but many of the original omissions made by Motte, who was afraid of legal prosecution because of some of the allegorical references, remained. In 1735, George Faulkner, a Dublin printer, issued an edition of *Gulliver's Travels* which included the passages omitted by Motte. One important section was omitted, however, by all of the eighteenth-century publishers. This passage, which concerned the rebellion of the people of Lindalino (Dublin) against the Wood coinage proposal, occurs near the end of the third chapter in the "Voyage to Laputa." This material, omitted intentionally by Motte and probably inadvertently by Faulkner, was not included in editions of *Gulliver's Travels* until the last decade of the nineteenth century. The Faulkner text of 1735, with the addition of the Wood coinage passage, is generally taken to be the best text of *Gulliver*, but Professor Arthur Case, an eminent Swift scholar, favors the Motte 1727 text.

Reception

Gulliver's Travels, written at the peak of Swift's powers, was in many ways the crowning achievement of his career as a satirist. The book, an unqualified success (its popularity demands comparison with today's best-sellers), was read from "cabinet council to nursery" and was even taken as the gospel truth in more than one quarter of the realm. It would be an exaggeration to suggest that the majority of Swift's contemporaries believed Gulliver's stories to be literally true, but there were a small handful who swallowed his solemn reports hook, line and sinker. Some claimed direct acquaintance with Gulliver himself, and others confirmed the geographical charts that Gulliver had so faithfully reproduced and Swift so fancifully fabricated. For the general public, however, the appeal of the book rested mainly on its satiric content and its associations with certain literature of the time.

By writing *Gulliver's Travels*, Swift made sure that he would belong to neither England nor Ireland, but to the world. And it is through Gulliver that the world knows Swift, even though many of his other works — *The Drapier's Letters, A Tale of a Tub, An Argument against Abolishing Christianity*, to name but three — must be counted among the literary triumphs of the English language.

Gulliver's Travels owed its power to the fact that it was the work of a writer who had been using satire as his medium for over a quarter of a century. His life had been one of continual disappointment and satire was his complaint and his defence — against his enemies and against mankind. Men, he believed, were generally ridiculous and petty, greedy and proud; they were blind to the "ideal of the mean." This ideal of the mean was present in one of Swift's first major satires, *The Battle of the Books* (1697). There, Swift took the side of the Ancients, but he showed their views to be ultimately as distorted as those of their adversaries, the Moderns. In Gulliver's last adventure, Swift again pointed to the ideal of the mean by positioning Gulliver between symbols of reason and symbols of sensuality. To Swift, man was a mixture of sense and nonsense; he had accomplished much but had fallen far short of what he could have been and what he could have done. In *Gulliver's Travels*, Swift made his strongest and most compelling statement on the position of man. The instant success of the book is due to the fact that this complex statement is couched in a fiction of rare artistry and marvellous imagination.

Swift's Sources and Motives

Gulliver's Travels is, in its form, a travel book. Accounts of travels, voyages both real and imaginary, enjoyed great popularity in Swift's time. Swift himself loved reading travellers' tales and the reports of explorers. In Temple's library at Moor Park, Swift "devoured" a great collection of them, and his affection for such writings made him the natural choice of the Scriblerus Club to produce the voyages of Martinus Scriblerus. If Pope's 1741 sketch of these travels represents what the Scriblerians had in mind, Swift realized their intention with striking success.

However, the Scriblerians shared the general skepticism of their age about the "legends of lying travellers." Swift's book tends to ridicule such works when Gulliver deals with them, and so Swift has cleverly managed to write a travel book while he is mocking its type. In preparing to write *Gulliver*, he filled himself with "I know not how many diverting books of history and travels," as he wrote to Vanessa. He made notes on Sir Thomas Herbert's *Some Yeares travaile . . . into Afrique & the greater Asia* as a preface to writing his own book.

Besides being influenced by the popular travel books of his time, Swift used as his sources such works as Cyrano de Bergerac's *Histoire comique de la lune* and his *Histoire du soleil*, Lucian's *True History*, and the writings of Rabelais and Tom Brown. The most thorough study of Swift's sources has been produced by Professor William A. Eddy (*Gulliver's Travels, A Critical Study*).

Of course, in addition to producing an interesting, amusing narrative, Swift had a didactic purpose in writing *Gulliver's Travels*. Didacticism was a characteristic quality of much eighteenth-century literature. The reader is not just supposed to be amused; he is also supposed to take the lessons of the book to heart. "For, who can read the Virtues I have mentioned in the glorious Houyhnhnms, without being ashamed of his own vices." This is just one of the many statements made by Gulliver in the *Travels*; yet, it demonstrates one of Swift's intentions. We are shown correct behavior; we are shown improper behavior. We are urged to emulate the former and to avoid the latter.

The first book of *Gulliver's Travels* was intended to satirize the Whigs and to defend the Tory ministry. Throughout the four books of *Gulliver*, Swift puts much emphasis on the political corruptions of his day. Swift believed that the governing power in a country should be balanced between three groups — the king or queen, the aristocrats and the commoners. Swift did not approve of political factions since he felt that political parties brought unnecessary divisions, jealousies and rivalries. It should be remembered that the much-praised king of Brobdingnag is a patriot monarch in a state without political parties. In addition, Swift was opposed to standing armies because he believed that such an army might overthrow proper political balance and place one political group in control. Yet, if the party system was to be carried on in England, Swift's sympathies were with the Tories.

The second book of *Gulliver's Travels* was designed to point out eighteenth-century political defects and corruptions. The state of England is contrasted with the politics in Brobdingnag and, from this contrast European statecraft, laws and government are seen in all their weakness and trickery.

The third voyage, which has been considered the weakest part of the *Travels* because it is so diffuse and episodic, satirizes several things; among these are the Royal Society, pedantry, speculation and interest in extreme "projects" in government and related areas, historians, literary commentators, and the desire for immortality on earth.

"A Voyage to the Country of the Houyhnhnms," the fourth book, levels its principal attack on man's sense of pride. Swift analyzes the characteristics of man's pride and some of its origins. In this section, Swift asks how man, corrupt, evil, irrational and deficient in so many things, can have the gall to possess the least ounce of pride. Thus, both the ordinary man and the Stoic, who glorified pride, are censured for being proud.

The bulk of the political allegory and most of the particular satiric references to individuals and happenings occur in Parts I and III, while "A Voyage to Brobdingnag" and "A Voyage to the Country of the Houyhnhnms" are more general in satiric purpose. Swift continually shifts his satiric and allegorical references. Thus, in some places he is allegorical; in other places he is not. His intention was to entertain as well as to teach, and this intention could be best fulfilled without sustained allegory and satire.

Satire, which may be defined as the ridiculing of vice and folly, was extremely popular in Augustan England. Neoclassic satirists believed that they could help to correct political, social, and moral faults by demonstrating the foolishness and vileness of the practices which were to be condemned. In order to achieve its purpose, satire usually makes use of comedy, wit, sarcasm and irony. Swift was a master of irony; that is, a master of saying one thing and meaning the reverse. In *A Modest Proposal*, for example, in which he suggests that Irish economic destitution might be solved by having the poor sell their children to butchers for meat, his irony becomes so intense that the horror of the situation burns itself into the reader's mind.

Since the government was particularly sensitive to criticism, many of the satirists of Swift's time cloaked their references to contemporary events and personages in allegory. Swift made considerable use of allegory in *Gulliver's Travels*. While most of the allegorical references

13

were undoubtedly obvious to Swift's contemporaries, some of the allusions have been lost in the course of time, and the meaning of other has been debated by scholars.

Beside certain aspects of the allegory, other elements of Swift' masterpiece have also been debated. Principal among these is Swift' alleged misanthrophy. For many years Swift's so-called misanthrophy has been stressed and condemned by some critics and commentators. That misanthrophy, to some degree, was a part of Swift's make-up could probably not be denied, but the tendency to push this personal trai forward as an "explanation" of the novel is misguided and non-pro ductive. Swift's comment, in a letter to Alexander Pope, should be recalled:

> I have ever hated all nations, professions, and communities, and all my love is toward individuals: for instance, I hate the tribe of lawyers, but I love Counsellor Such-a-one, and Judge Such-a-one: so with physicians — I will not speak of my own trade — soldiers, English, Scotch, French, and the rest. But principally I hate and detest that animal called man, although I heartily love John, Peter, Thomas, and so forth.

Gulliver does, of course, at the end of his last voyage reach a state of misanthrophy. But, as many scholars have pointed out, Gulliver does not represent Swift when the former becomes misanthropic. Swift demon strates that Gulliver's final attitude is not logical by showing the kind ness of the Portuguese ship captain, Don Pedro de Mendez, and by making fun of Gulliver's conduct on the voyage home and when he returns to his wife and family. It has, in fact, become so common to emphasize misanthrophy in the fourth voyage that several critics have recently had to indicate the rich vein of comedy which exists in the "Voyage to the Country of the Houyhnhnms," along with a harrowing pessimism.

During Swift's time, several philosophers and thinkers — such as Anthony Ashley Cooper, the third earl of Shaftesbury — emphasized the natural goodness of man and stressed a rational and benevolent optimism. Swift, however, grounded in Christian theology as it pertains to man's evil nature and the doctrine of original sin, did not believe in man's "goodness," and he was bent on showing man as he believed man to be: weak, corrupt, but with rational potential to improve his lot. This interpretation of Swift's attitude has been advanced by T. O. Wedel, Louis A. Landa and several other Swift scholars, and would seem to be the most logical explanation of Swift's pessimism. It should not be forgotten that Swift was a clergyman in the Church of England. His sermons and pamphlets on religious matters confirm his belief in Anglican theology and his antagonism to Deism. Swift was opposed to

eism principally because he felt that the Deists, by rejecting Biblical
nd revealed religion (which sets up moral restraints), gave themselves
stification for any improper behavior. (See the excellent essay entitled
Church and State" in Ricardo Quintana's book *The Mind and Art of
onathan Swift*.)

One of the most noticeable features of the *Travels* is Swift's atten-
on to minute details and his realistic touches. We are told where
ulliver lives in England; we are told about his wife and children; we
e given detailed descriptions of his adventures and of the people and
aces he visits. As a result, a considerable amount of genuine credibility
generated.

The reader of *Gulliver's Travels* should also keep in mind the
nportance to Swift of morality and common sense. He was acutely
onscious of the faults coming from man's passions. Swift was opposed
excess or "enthusiasm" in any form — in politics, in science, or in
ligion. In *Gulliver's Travels*, he wished, among other things, to show
at man was not an *"animal rationale"* but *"rationis capax."* (That is,
ot a rational animal but an animal *capable* of reason.) Swift added that
e would never "have peace of mind till all honest men are of my
pinion." No reader of *Gulliver's Travels* could deny that it is a powerful
ustration in favor of Swift's opinion.

Plot Summary

A physician named Lemuel Gulliver takes a position as ship
doctor on the *Antelope*, which embarks from Bristol in May, 169?
heading for the South Seas. But, near Tasmania, the ship is wrecked by
storm. Swimming for his life, Gulliver is carried by wind and tid?
fortunately, to a shore, where, in sheer exhaustion, he falls asleep.

Waking, he finds himself tied to the ground by several hundred tin
ropes. Humans six inches tall have imprisoned him by this method. H?
captors feed him. Then, still bound, he is put in a wagon that has bee?
built especially for him, drawn by fifteen hundred horses on the sam?
scale as the diminutive human natives. He is carried to the capital city ?
Lilliput, as this strange land is called. There, he is exhibited as a?
enormous curiosity piece to the tiny, gaping citizens. Then he is chaine?
to a (comparatively) huge building, in which there is space, if he crawl?
for sheltered sleep at night.

Gradually, as the days pass, the naturally curious Gulliver learn?
the language of the land. Since he is a charming and polished man, ?
gentlemanly habits, he becomes a fixture in the royal court, favored b?
the Lilliputian emperor and made much of by the court ladies. Even?
tually the emperor grants him freedom from captivity provided that h?
follows an intricately drawn pattern of rules in his behavior. The free?
Gulliver tours Lilliput's capital city, Mildendo, and marvels at i?
similarity to the cities of his far-away Europe.

Blefuscu, a neighboring empire, threatens to invade Lilliput. Gu?
liver volunteers to save Lilliput, and his emperor gratefully accepts th?
man-mountain's services. Only eight hundred yards separate the tw?
empires, and the navy of Blefuscu is waiting for favorable winds to se?
sail and invade Lilliput. But Gulliver simply wades across to Blefusc?
and drags back the entire enemy fleet by attaching their ships to hooke?
cables. The joyous emperor confers nobility on Gulliver, who is cele?
brated for his feat.

When Gulliver, however, discovers that the emperor intends t?
enslave the conquered people of Blefuscu, he protests, defending th?
principles of liberty. The issue is taken up by the Lilliputian parliamen?
where Gulliver's liberal sentiments win out, resulting in a peace settle?
ment fair to Blefuscu. But now the emperor and court of Lilliput resen?
Gulliver, who, for his successful interference, has fallen into disfavor.

Gulliver pays a visit to Blefuscu, whose emperor and people ha?
him graciously. While exploring this land, he happens to discover a shi?
that had washed ashore. The artisans of Blefuscu help him to repair thi?
Gulliver-size boat, so that he can finally return home to England. H?
puts some tiny cattle and sheep on board, and sets sail on his homewar?
voyage. An English vessel picks him up, and he is soon reunited with h?
English family, in an old and normal world. But home, apparently, ?

not for him. After two months he ships out again, bound for India, on the *Adventure*.

Strong winds blow Gulliver's ship off course to Great Tartary, where a landing party goes ashore to forage for supplies. The curious Gulliver wanders away from his mates. When an enormous giant chases the others back to the ship, Gulliver finds himself left behind, on this strange island. He hides in a field where the grain is forty feet high. There, a farmer's family, out threshing, discovers him. They make him their pet, for his diminutive, humanlike characteristics afford the giants great amusement. The farmer's daughter, who, though only nine years old, stands almost forty feet high, takes charge of him. Gulliver has become her adorable, tiny, animate doll.

Gulliver is now a showpiece, displayed at the local market town, to the profit of his farmer captor. Then he is brought to the huge metropolis and put on show. These enforced exertions tax his health. The shrewd farmer, seeing that his pet would die at this rate, sells him to the queen of Brobdingnag. Gulliver becomes quite a celebrated curiosity, striking the fancy of the queen and her court. Doctors and philosophers of the court make an exacting, "scientific" study of the diminutive Gulliver, whom they regard as a freak of nature, a rare cosmic eccentricity.

By being so oddly out of proportion in this oversized land, Gulliver is persecuted by natural hazards and terrors. In a marvelous series of adventures, he finds himself endangered, in turn, by lion-sized rats, a thirty-foot-high dwarf, partridge-size wasps, barrel-sized apples, and tennis ball-sized hailstones. Each time, he makes good his escape, after considerable anxiety.

The king of Brobdingnag questions Gulliver about Great Britain. Gulliver is reduced to shame for his native land in trying to answer these questions truthfully. He finds that he can defend the honor and integrity of social institutions and political practices in his homeland only by resorting to evasive lies. This conflict between his veracity and his patriotic loyalty embarrasses him. Brobdingnag's institutions, as described by the king, are comparatively fairer and saner, and logically require no defence for their moral existence. Gulliver is thus made to feel totally inferior, not only as a tiny, helpless human, but as a no-longer-justifiably-proud citizen of England. Not only does he find his physical stature too small, but also his moral and social identity as a subject of his state.

Gulliver endures two years in this terrifying land of the giants. Then, miraculously, a great bird swoops down, snatches up Gulliver's portable box-residence (with Gulliver occupying it), and carries it over the sea. There it is dropped and floats aimlessly. Ultimately, an England-bound ship sights Gulliver and rescues him. Back in England, it takes Gulliver a long time to become accustomed to the normal, "tiny"

17

sizes of people and things, in a world now viewed with a different perspective.

Gulliver cannot stay put at home. He sets to sea again. The ship is attacked by Chinese pirates, who leniently cast Gulliver adrift on a sailboat. It carries him to a rocky island. A large floating mass — the flying island of Laputa — descends from the sky. Gulliver boards it, and it ascends again. Gulliver discovers that Laputa's inhabitants are all absent-minded intellectuals perpetually floundering in the airy realm of the impractical and the abstract. These citizens, their king included, have to be followed about by servants who remind them what courses their abstruse conversations have been taking. Absorbed in abstract sciences, the Laputans are completely unable to cope with practical, everyday concerns of life. They cannot even make clothes that fit them, yet their telescopes are so fine that they have discovered many new stars. Even their infidelities are so absent-minded that their wives don't bother to complain or even feel much resentment.

The floating island empire of Laputa enforces obedience on a subject colony, Balnibarbi, which Gulliver visits. For forty years, this land has been infected with the enthusiasm for occult "science," derived contagiously from the Laputans. The inhabitants of Balnibarbi pursue absurd projects instead of useful arts. They are in rags, their cities are in ruins, they neglect productive architecture, in a madness that has apparently infected the whole population. But they seem to disregard with indifference, the inconveniences and consequential discomforts that spring from their fanatical theorizing. They don't see their own world, but another one, the product of disjointed fantasy.

Gulliver tours the Grand Academy. Loosely based, ill-founded projects for improving agriculture and building are in progress, with hilarious ineffectuality. The "useful" artists of the Grand Academy of Balnibarbi are occupied in such activities as extracting sunbeams from cucumbers, resolving human excrement, calcinating ice into gunpowder, and softening marble for pillows. Projectors in speculative learning are trying to compose books from a preposterous machine. Projectors in the school of languages are busy trying to abolish words and conversing by means of things. Projectors in the mathematical school attempt to acquire theorems by ingurgitation. In the school of political projectors, the professors grapple with visionary schemes for wise and honest government. Certain medical treatment for members of political assemblies is proposed. To be prevented from indulging their vice of forgetfulness, ministers should be tweaked by the nose, kicked in the belly, or tread on the corns. After delivering their opinions, senators should be required to vote contrary to them. Skulls of the members of conflicting political parties should be split in half and exchanged, so that governmental solidarity might ensue. To apprehend plots, the diet and excrement of the suspects should be put under scrutiny.

Gulliver takes a boat journey to an island of sorcerers, Glubbdub-drib. Its governor magically conjures up, to Gulliver's amazed observation, the apparitions of Alexander, Hannibal, Caesar, Pompey, Sir Thomas More, Socrates, Plato, Aristotle, and other great figures of history. By talking with them, Gulliver learns not to trust the standard history books, with whose texts and apparently erroneous suppositions the speeches of the apparitions conflict. For example, Homer and Aristotle disown their commentators, and Aristotle predicts that the recent Newtonian system will be eventually rejected. In general, classical history is defended as true, and modern history as false.

Having had enough of Glubbdubdrib, Gulliver visits Luggnagg, whose king welcomes him and shows him the Struldbruggs, Luggnaggian immortals, doomed never to die. At first, Gulliver wants to stay forever on this land, for he has equated indefinitely extended longevity with human superiority. But he is soon disillusioned when he discovers how inferior the Struldbruggs have been made by the dubious endowment of immortality. They are not, as he had expected, men of accumulated wisdom "who being exempt from that universal calamity of human nature have their minds free and disengaged without the weight and depression of spirits caused by the continual apprehension of death." The infirmities of age are merely perpetuated, on the contrary, and a Struldbrugg's highest happiness is to be relieved from consciousness by an escape into the oblivion of senility. Death, Gulliver comes to realize, is actually a blessing, not an evil, of Providence.

Gulliver journeys on to Japan, then ships back to England, from which he has been absent for three years.

As usual, before long Gulliver wants to leave England again for some distant unknown territory. He signs as ship's captain, sailing, in 1710, for the South Seas. But the crew mutinies, imprisoning Gulliver in his cabin for several months. Then he is set adrift off an unknown coast. On coming ashore, he encounters, to his disgust, some abominable creatures, half-ape, half-human, who revolt him, but who flee in terror when they sight a horse.

Gulliver comes to realize the conditions prevailing in the amazing land. Rational horses, called Houyhnhnms, are the masters of irrational "humans," called Yahoos. Taken in by a Houyhnhnm family, Gulliver lives in a stable with a diet of oaten cake and milk. When he reveals to his hosts the fact that, in England, horses are used as beasts of burden by Yahoo-like creatures, the Houyhnhnms are horrified. Gulliver's description of the social practices prevalent in England mystifies the Houyhnhnms, whose straightforward, candid natures can hardly comprehend such outlandish notions as wars and law courts. This benevolent race of intelligent horses is appalled by Gulliver's explanations of the institutions of his native land, which seem "inhuman" to them.

Gulliver is delighted to live among these eminently rational horses.

But his contented existence with them ends when his host reluctantly informs him what the Grand Assembly of the Houyhnhnms has decided as to Gulliver's fate: either he must be treated as an ordinary Yahoo (which would incur a tremendous deflation of his ego and a loss of all dignity, pretended or real); or he must swim back to the land he came from.

Gulliver builds a canoe and sadly sails away. A Portuguese vessel, heading for Lisbon, picks him up. Its sailors disgust Gulliver — who had been spoiled by the great nobility of the Houyhnhnms — with their gross reminders of the despised Yahoos. He becomes a recluse on the ship, hating all of mankind. But the ship's captain, a kind and sympathetic man named Don Pedro, treats Gulliver with humanity and compassion, recognizing that this Englishman has just emerged from some shattering experience.

From Lisbon, Gulliver sails to England. But when he meets his family, who greet him with innocent and unsuspecting joy, he is repulsed. A kiss from his own wife makes him faint. Now, for this melancholy, disillusioned man, only horses can be his friends. He has learned to see humans as the beastly things they are, and is purged of love for them forever. He settles down to his sobered misanthropy, for his strange experiences have mortified all pride in being that thing called man.

Characters and Places in the Novel

The Publisher to the Reader

LEMUEL GULLIVER: The author of the *Travels*, a native of Nottinghamshire.

MARY BURTON GULLIVER: Edmond Burton's daughter, whom Gulliver married after his voyage on the *Swallow*.

RICHARD SYMPSON: Gulliver's fictional cousin who prevailed upon Gulliver to publish the *Travels*.

Book I

JAMES BATES: A London surgeon under whom young Gulliver studied medicine.

ABRAHAM PANNELL: The master of the *Swallow*, the ship in which Gulliver first went to sea as a ship's surgeon.

WILLIAM PRICHARD: The master of the *Antelope*, a ship which sank in the vicinity of Lilliput.

GOLBASTO MOMAREN EVLAME GURDILO SHEFIN MULLY ULLY GUE: The emperor of Lilliput.

FLIMNAP: Lord High Treasurer of Lilliput.

RELDRESAL: A Lilliputian councillor, Principal Secretary of Private Affairs.

SKYRESH BOLGOLAM: High admiral of Lilliput, a counsellor of the Emperor.

SLAMECKSAN: A Lilliputian political party, the Low Heels.

TRAMECKSAN: A Lilliputian political party, the High Heels.

NARDAC: The title of nobility conferred on Gulliver by the emperor of Lilliput.

JOHN BIDDEL: The master of the vessel that picks up Gulliver after he leaves Lilliput.

LILLIPUT: An island near Van Diemen's Land (Tasmania), inhabited by a race of people six inches high.

MILDENDO: The capital city of Lilliput.

BELFABORAC: The royal palace of Lilliput.

BLEFUSCU: A neighboring island of Lilliput; a refuge for Big Endian exiles.

Book II

JOHN NICHOLAS: The master of the *Adventure*, the vessel that carried Gulliver to Brobdingnag.

BROBDINGNAG: A land inhabited by a race of giants possessing great moral stature.

GLUMDALCLITCH: Gulliver's nurse; the daughter of Gulliver's master in Brobdingnag.

FLANFLASNIC: The site of the palace of the king of Brobdingnag.

LORBRULGRUD: The capital city of Brobdingnag, the "Pride of the Universe."

GRILDRIG: Gulliver's name in Brobdingnag.

SPLACKNUCK: An animal found in Brobdingnag, about six feet long, resembling a human being.

THOMAS WILCOCKS: The master of the vessel that rescues Gulliver after he is carried away from Brobdingnag by an eagle.

Book III

CAPTAIN WILLIAM ROBINSON: The master of the *Hopewell*, the ship on which Gulliver sails to the waters of Laputa.

LAPUTA: The flying island inhabited by a race of impractical visionaries.

CLIMENOLE: A Laputan domestic appointed to arouse his master to reality.

BALNIBARBI: An island subject to the rule of the Laputan king.

MUNODI: The governor of Lagado, on Balnibarbi.

LINDALINO: A city that rebelled against the authority of the Laputan monarch.

LAGADO: A city on Balnibarbi; capital of the kingdom of Laputa.

GLUBBDUBDRIB: An island of sorcerers.

LUGGNAGG: The land where the immortal Struldbruggs live.

STRULDBRUGGS: A race of humans who age without dying; they are immortal but their immortality has none of its supposed delights.

THEORORUS VANGRULT: The captain of the *Amboyna*, the vessel on which Gulliver sails from Japan to Amsterdam.

Book IV

CAPTAIN POCOCK: The commanding officer of the ship that accompanied Gulliver's vessel at the outset of the last voyage.

HOUYHNHNMS: Superior, totally rational horses, who are the masters of the Yahoos.

YAHOOS: The repugnant man-like creatures held in subjection by the Houyhnhnms.

PEDRO DE MENDEZ: The kindly captain of the Portuguese ship that rescues Gulliver; he aids Gulliver to return to England.

Chapter by Chapter Summaries and Commentaries

THE PUBLISHER TO THE READER

Summary

This is a preface signed by "an ancient and intimate friend" and relative of Mr. Gulliver's, Richard Sympson. He tells of places where Gulliver has lived before settling in his present home near Newark, in Nottinghamshire, and of how Gulliver became a test of truth with his former neighbors at Redriff, who "proved" the truth of what they said by affirming that it "was as true as if Mr. Gulliver spoke it." Sympson as publisher commends the "air of truth" in Gulliver's account of the travels, mentions that he has edited out innumerable details from the book, and invites the reader to examine the original manuscript for himself if he wishes to do so.

Commentary

Sympson's letter should not be overlooked as a part of Gulliver's travel book. It seeks to secure *verisimilitude* (seeming truth) for the author and his account of his adventures. Swift cleverly suggests that Gulliver is a real person and his story is true. The reader may talk to Gulliver's former neighbors at Redriff or his present ones near Newark. He may examine the Gulliver tombs at Banbury, question Gulliver himself, or examine the omitted details (which would tend to confirm the story as Gulliver gave it) in the original book Gulliver sent to the publisher. There is, Sympson thus implies, no fiction, no hoax here.

Book I — A Voyage to Lilliput

CHAPTER 1

Summary

Gulliver announces himself as the third son of five, born to his Nottinghamshire parents. When three years' study at Cambridge had exhausted his father's ability to maintain him there, Gulliver was made apprentice to Mr. Bates, a London surgeon. Along with his medical studies, Gulliver pursued navigation and "other parts of the mathematics" useful to those who intend to travel. After four years with Mr. Bates, Gulliver received backing from his family to study medicine at Leyden University. Next, he served under Captain Abraham Pannell as surgeon to the ship, *Swallow*. He married Mary Burton, daughter of a hosier in Newgate Street, London, who brought with her four hundred pounds as dowry. But his medical practice in London did badly. Gulliver went back to sea for several voyages. At last, he sailed May 4, 1699, on the *Antelope*, under Captain William Pritchard, to the South Seas. Near Van Diemen's Land (Tasmania), the ship was driven violently north-west by a storm and wrecked. Of six who were thrown into the water from an overturning lifeboat, only Gulliver managed to swim until he could touch bottom and wade ashore. Exhausted, he fell into a profound sleep.

Gulliver awoke to find his arms, legs, and hair fastened to the ground and himself a prisoner of a nation of little men, six inches high (the Lilliputians, as he later learned). When he seemed on the point of breaking free from his bonds, the tiny people discharged such a volley of stinging arrows at him that he thought it more prudent to lie still until night should bring a better opportunity to escape. The Lilliputians erected a platform, from which a little person, evidently of great importance, directed a long address at Gulliver, who could make nothing of it. But the orator understood Gulliver's signs indicating that he was hungry. By the speaker's orders, little ladders were set up against Gulliver's sides and delicious meats and wine were brought to him. After this hospitality Gulliver felt bound, as a guest, not to hurt those who thus entertained him.

Influenced by a drug that had been put into his wine, Gulliver soon fell asleep again. He awoke this time bound to a sort of low wagon on which these ingenious minute people, using fifteen hundred of the king's horses, were drawing Gulliver into their capital, Mildendo. In the city, he was housed in an abandoned temple, thought to be the largest in the kingdom, but no longer put to sacred use because of an unnatural murder committed there some years before. To this building Gulliver was chained by one leg, but left free enough to enter and to leave his quarters. Gulliver, a national wonder, was viewed by thousands.

Commentary

Swift continues the effort to secure verisimilitude. Gulliver studies at Cambridge. He goes to Leyden, the leading medical university in Europe. Presumably, any reader could obtain real information on Gulliver from the officers of these universities, and his friends at each would remember him. He sails under captains and in ships whose records can be checked. His father-in-law's name and business address are given. Lilliput becomes a part of the real world because it is reached exactly as any other part of the real world is reached: one boards an English ship in an English port and sails under an English captain until one arrives at Lilliput. Perhaps, at the moment, Gulliver thinks nothing of the fact that the Lilliputian sea is so shallow that he can touch bottom a mile from shore or that the grass in which he sleeps is "very soft and short;" but both "facts" are appropriate to the little people and the little land he has come to visit. To help preserve the illusion of reality, Lilliput (like the other lands of the voyages) is placed on a part of the map still in Swift's time left blank because as yet it was unexplored.

Swift keeps everything in Lilliput proportionate to the six-inch size of his tiny people. Thus, what look like shoulders and loins of mutton at Gulliver's meal are smaller than the wings of an English lark; the tallest trees are seven feet high; the large gate of the kingdom's largest temple building is four feet high and two wide.

Swift's Lilliputian words — *tolgo phonac, Langro dehul san, Hurgo,* and so on — have led several scholars to believe that Swift constructed the languages of his exotic lands on careful principles. Traditionally, however, these languages have been regarded as examples of Swift's well-known love of verbal nonsense and wordplay. To pursue this subject, interested students may like to see Swift's *A Proposal for Correcting . . . the English Language* (addressed to Robert Harley) or *A Gulliver Dictionary* by Paul Odell.

The "unnatural murder" mentioned above is thought to refer to the execution of that "royal holy martyr," the "sainted" Charles I in 1649. And the large polluted temple, consequently, would be Westminster Abbey, where Charles was condemned to die. Swift's Church and Tory sympathies lay naturally with King Charles.

CHAPTER 2

Summary

Gulliver saw around Mildendo a country beautifully arranged and cultivated — "like a continued garden." But he himself had an unlovely and embarrassing problem of how to escape the crowds and "disburthen" himself of an uneasy excremental accumulation of two days. He solved his problem by creeping into his temple house and emerged to find the royal family of Lilliput present to visit with him. The emperor, taller than all others in his court, seemed to be a noble, energetic and courageous prince. Unable, despite Gulliver's wide acquaintance with languages and the efforts of the court scholars, to find a tongue they knew in common, the emperor and his huge guest nevertheless got on well together.

Gulliver, now a Lilliputian national problem, became the subject of much high-level debate. What should be done if the man-mountain should break loose? Would maintaining him empty the treasury or cause famine in the land? Should he be starved to death? Poisoned? Would so large a carcass cause a plague in the city and spread to the whole country? Fortunately for Gulliver, his show of leniency to six soldiers who had been delivered up to him for shooting at him with arrows impressed the emperor and his council with Gulliver's good will. They sent out to the nation detailed orders about supplying the needs of the man-mountain, assigned hundreds of Lilliputians as his servants at national expense, and named six leading scholars to teach him their language. Their huge guest, a natural master of languages, made prodigious strides in learning. His first request — for his liberty — the emperor was not yet ready to grant. With Gulliver's consent, he had two officers search Gulliver and make a detailed inventory of what they found in his pockets. (The inventory is translated and delivered to the reader in the text.) When the emperor requested a show of Gulliver's weapons, the man-mountain surprised and terrified the Lilliputians first by waving his shining scimitar in the sun and then by discharging a pistol.

Commentary

Swift's frequent presentation of natural functions, seen in this chapter, in Chapter 1, and in other places in the *Travels*, has been much and variously commented on. As part of a book aimed at battling man's pride, this kind of passage reminds man that, insist how he will upon having rationality, he *is* an animal. Swift forever railed against man's romantic misconceptions of himself, as he does here and in some of his poems: "A Beautiful Young Nymph going to Bed;" "The Lady's Dressing Room;" "Strephon and Chloe," and some others.

Since Swift's day, the emperor of Lilliput has been taken to represent, in some ways, George I of England. But there is some irony in the presentation, since Swift did not find George admirable. Perhaps the author was also guarding himself against legal troubles. Before publishing the book, he wrote of having difficulty finding a printer willing to risk his ears (for printers of treasonable material were punished with the loss of those appendages). In making the emperor an awesome figure to his people because he towered above them nearly the breadth of a fingernail, Swift ridicules the "difference" between the politically great and small. Kings rarely exhibit real superiority over other men; indeed, they are often not even the natural equals of others. How well would most kings do in the Olympic Games, or in arts, or in sciences, or in managing a giant corporation? Accidental distinction of birth confers no natural superiority.

The reader should constantly watch Gulliver's reactions in terms of his character. At *this* point in the story, he is fairly simple-minded, unsophisticated, easy-going, unsuspicious. He makes much of his ex-cremental difficulties, as if they had importance compared with many other details of his interesting and *dangerous* situation in Lilliput. He is ready to be pleased — with the lovely country about Mildendo, for example. He does no lasting harm to the six soldiers who had shot at him, although he uses them as a warning against further aggression by suggesting that he might eat them if he chose. He accepts the face value of the Lilliputians' apparent good will. But by his unruffled report of what went on in the emperor's council, Gulliver — or rather Swift, over

Gulliver's unsuspecting head — acquaints us with the Lilliputians' capacity for treachery and sneakiness.

The search of Gulliver's pockets has at least two meanings. It is an amusing "example" of how people can misconceive and misinterpret matters unfamiliar to them. (The searchers take Gulliver's watch to be an unknown animal or a god or an oracle.) On that level, the search belongs to a children's story. On a deeper satiric level, the search has always reminded readers of the Whigs' diligent search into the public and private affairs of the Tories after Queen Anne's death, and the constructions they put on what they found. The Whigs hoped to destroy the Tory leaders, Swift's friends, Harley, St. John (Bolingbroke) and their colleagues, by discovering treason in Tory efforts to end the War of the Spanish Succession in 1711-13, and in Tory contacts with the court of the Stuart pretender to the English throne.

CHAPTER 3

Summary

Hoping for his freedom, Gulliver carefully nourished the Lilliputians' trust in him. He found Lilliputian court entertainments admirable for their dexterity and magnificence, being particularly impressed by the skill of dancers vying for high office by trying to jump higher than anyone else without falling from a suspended rope. By far the most skilful in this art was Flimnap, the treasurer; but even he once took a fall which would have broken his neck if one of the king's cushions had not, luckily, been lying in a position to save him. Another contest, for which the prizes were silken threads of blue, red, and green, tested the skill of candidates in leaping over or creeping under a stick held by the emperor.

Gulliver in his turn entertained the court. He allowed the emperor's cavalry to test their horses' prowess by jumping them over a Gulliverian hand or foot, or to perform military exercises on his handkerchief after he had suspended it on four sticks to make a little stage of it. At the emperor's request he stood like a colossus with legs apart while the Lilliputian army staged a grand parade beneath him. Contrary to orders, some of the younger officers found much to laugh about by looking up through the rents in Gulliver's breeches.

By this time, the granting of Gulliver's liberty was opposed by only one lord in the council, Skyresh Bolgolam, Admiral of the Realm, who for no known reason considered Gulliver a personal enemy. But Bolgolam gave his consent in exchange for being allowed to dictate the terms on which Gulliver should be freed. The conditions, eight in number, specified that in various ways Gulliver not disrupt the traffic and operations of the kingdom, not leave the kingdom without official license, be available six days a month for emergency express duty, assist in the war against the island of Blefuscu, help in managing certain great stones for royal building projects, and deliver within two months a survey of the circumference of Lilliput. For these considerations the man-mountain was to have daily meat and drink enough to nourish 1,728 Lilliputians and have free access to the royal person and other marks of favor.

Commentary

Flimnap represents Robert Walpole, whose official position was, like Flimnap's, that of treasurer. But, in fact (not in name), he became the first prime minister in English history, leading the Whig government and dominating English policy for twenty-one years (1721-42). After the death of Queen Anne, he had been chairman of the committee to impeach Swift's Tory friends, and Swift enjoyed satirizing Walpole, who is here ridiculed as politically agile but still a *mere* politician. The king's cushion represents the Duchess of Kendal, one of King George I's mistresses, whom Walpole was believed to have bribed in order to return to power in 1721. The three threads represent the three British Royal Orders of the Garter, the Bath, and the Thistle, here presented as rewards for contemptible subservience, leaping and creeping at the whim of the prince. Walpole influenced George I to revive the Order of the Bath in 1725 as being, or so the Tories jeered, a thrifty means of paying off political debts.

Gulliver continues to be naïve and uncritical. He gives no sign of recognizing that rope-dancing and leaping and creeping are poor tests for responsible government positions or for honors from a royal hand. Neither does he suggest that such postures and exercises ill befit the dignity of great officers. Thus, the satire early in the *Travels* is free from the bitterness that will develop as Gulliver begins to perceive corruption and contemptibility in mankind.

Swift will not relent in his war on man's pride. Just when Gulliver may seem to be at a peak of superiority, as now, he is made to appear a fool and reminded of his animal grossness by the laughter of the soldiers beneath him.

Skyresh Bolgolam, "of a morose and sour complexion," is a Swiftian creation designed to ridicule the Earl of Nottingham, once (1680-84) First Lord of the Admiralty, whom Swift had lampooned as "Dismal" in some ballads in 1711. Nottingham had referred to Swift in parliament as a clergyman "hardly suspected of being a Christian," yet still "in a fair way of being a Bishop."

Swift continues to expose the foolishness of man's pride. Bolgolam, six inches tall, displays astonishing presumption in adopting Gulliver as a personal enemy. Similarly, the Lilliputian nation haughtily presumes to bind Gulliver with niggling conditions in the treaty. Clearly, they have no sense of their own puny impotence against such power as Gulliver could bring to bear against them. The Lilliputians have giant-sized vices.

The Lilliputian emperor also has giant-sized titles. The pretentiousness of the titles worn by this snippet of a creature contrasts laughably not only with his size but also, as will be noted later, with the title of the huge and good Brobdingnagian, who was not even an emperor, and by no means "monarch of all monarchs" nor "His most sublime Majesty," but only a king. Swift mocks not only the presumptuous and inflated titles of earthly kings but every man's tendency to take himself too seriously.

CHAPTER 4

Summary

Gulliver's first project after regaining his freedom was to inspect the city of Mildendo. The city was an exact square, 500 feet on each side, enclosed by a wall two-and-a-half feet high and 11 inches wide. Its streets were regularly laid out, with the palace buildings rising five feet high in the center of the city. By making two stools to stand on, Gulliver was able to step into the palace enclosure and inspect it.

Two weeks later, Reldresal, principal secretary of private affairs, visited Gulliver. Lilliput, he explained, suffered from two serious evils: danger of invasion from the rival kingdom of Blefuscu and internal dangers from political divisions between the high heels, or *Tramecksan*, and the low heels, or *Slamecksan*.

These domestic divisions were involved with a related quarrel between Big Endians and Little Endians, a quarrel dating back to an edict of the present Lilliputian emperor's grandfather ordering the people under severest penalties to break their eggs at the smaller end instead of at the larger end as tradition had always dictated. Resistance to this innovation had caused six rebellions, in which one emperor had lost his life and another his crown, and 11,000 Lilliputians had died. The emperors of Blefuscu, calling the new manner of breaking eggs a fundamental religious error, had for generations received Big Endian exiles from Lilliput, cherished them, and stood ready to help them reimpose the ancient discipline on Little Endian Lilliput. For 36 moons (months), Reldresal reported, a costly and bloody war had been raging over the question between the two nations, and at the moment Blefuscu was poised to strike at Lilliput with a powerful fleet. His Majesty of Lilliput, trusting in Gulliver's valor and strength, had desired his enormous guest to be informed of the state of affairs. Gulliver declined to take sides in party strife within the kingdom, but announced his readiness to defend the emperor and his state from all invaders.

Commentary

The excellent order and beauty of Mildendo increases the evidence of intelligence and ingenuity in the Lilliputians. They are great engineers and their city a model of city planning. Gulliver continues to show his simple, open nature, his readiness to admire what deserves admiration, and his freedom from envy of the successes of others. Whether intelligence in men guarantees moral integrity remains to be seen in the Lilliputian sequel.

The parties, Tramecksan and Slamecksan, as the reader easily sees, correspond to Tory (roughly High Church) and Whig (roughly Low Church) in England. The Lilliputian emperor favors the Slamecksan, as George I did the Whigs; but his son had friends in both camps — hence the hobble that results from his having one high and one low heel. The Prince of Wales (later George II) showed such ambiguous political leaning in England.

The Big Endians, of course, represent the Roman Catholics of England and the Little Endians the Protestants. Blefuscu stands for France, where Catholic and Tory exiles received refuge and assistance, where the exiled Stuart family maintained a court and stoutly insisted on their rights as the English royal family, and from which England received threats of invasion. Swift's Endian allegory briefly accounts for over 150 years of English history from the time of the Protestant break from Rome. Charles I would be the emperor who lost his life, James II the one who lost his throne. That Big Endians could not hold "employments" refers to the Test Act, which barred military and civil offices to all who failed to "take the Sacrament" in the Anglican church.

CHAPTER 5

Summary

Gulliver became a national hero. He studied the Blefuscudian fleet from across the 800-yard channel that separated the two little enemy kingdoms. He fashioned 50 hooks on little cables and, having swum and waded to the Blefuscudian shore, fastened a hook to each of the 50 men-of-war he found there. Recovering from their first terror of the giant invader, the Blefuscudians furiously rained arrows on Gulliver while he worked. He protected his eyes with his spectacles, and when all was ready he towed the fighting part of the fleet triumphantly to Lilliput. The emperor made him a Nardac (man of highest honor) on the spot. Gulliver, however, refused to co-operate in reducing Blefuscu to absolute slavery by capturing all the enemy's remaining ships and thus establish the Lilliputian emperor as sole monarch of what was considered to be the entire world. Gulliver protested that he "would never be an instrument of bringing a free and brave people into slavery."

Grievously offended by Gulliver's refusal, the emperor began to intrigue with a clique of ministers to bring Gulliver to harm. The man-mountain further alienated the emperor by certain friendly gestures towards the ambassadors from Blefuscu who arrived to make a treaty with Lilliput. He promptly and gladly accepted an invitation to visit the Blefuscudian court, but he noticed an unmistakable coldness in the Lilliputian emperor when Gulliver sought permission to carry out the visit. The coolness, he later discovered, sprang from the machinations of Flimnap and Bolgolam, who had persuaded the emperor that Gulliver's friendliness to the Blefuscudians signalled a disaffection for the emperor.

Gulliver next made an enemy of the empress. When her apartments were found burning in the night, the man-mountain, with admirable presence of mind, extinguished the fire by urinating upon it. But the empress, abhorring the methods of the Gulliverian fire-department, resolved that she would never again use the apartments and that she would have revenge on the fire chief.

Commentary

The capture of the fleet here suggests the Tory claims of having destroyed French naval power in the War of Spanish Succession. As a matter of policy, and to distract attention from the army successes of the Duke of Marlborough (Whig champion), the Tories systematically emphasized the fact that England was a naval, not a land power. Here, therefore, Gulliver represents the ministers Harley, Bolingbroke and their fellow Tories. Swift "uses" Gulliver at other times to represent different people. Gulliver's refusal to help in the complete destruction of Blefuscudian power suggests the Tory rejection of Whig demands to pursue the war to "total victory" and the annihilation of French power. Like Gulliver, the Tories were accused of irregularities and even treason in their dealings with the French preparatory to arranging the Treaty of Utrecht, 1713.

The empress's horror at Gulliver's well-intended help has usually been considered a reference to Queen Anne's horror of Swift's *A Tale of a Tub* and her consequent refusal to make him a bishop — all despite the fact that Swift's book supports Anne's Church of England against both Catholics and dissenters.

CHAPTER 6

Summary

Surveying the world of Lilliput, Gulliver found some of its laws and customs "peculiar" as being contrary to those of his own dear country. False accusers were put to death after the accused had proved their innocence, and those falsely accused were reimbursed four-fold from the accusers' estates for all charges and inconveniences of the trial. Fraud was thought a greater crime than theft, because it took advantage of trust, whereas one could easily guard against mere theft.

The Lilliputians rewarded keepers of the law just as they punished lawbreakers. Those who had kept the law for 73 moons received the title of *Snilpal*, or Legal. Government in this empire was considered a matter of ordinary intelligence and virtue, not one of genius. Genius in government, in fact, they feared, because high intelligence will enable a man to do more damage than will ordinary intelligence if he is disposed to evil; and a highly intelligent man can well defend himself against charges of wrongdoing. Disbelief in Providence barred a man from public office, for it seemed absurd to the Lilliputians to employ men who disowned the authority of which the emperor himself was a deputy.

To Lilliputians, ingratitude was a capital crime, for he who injured his benefactor must be an enemy to all men. They considered children under no obligation to parents for bringing them into the world, nor were parents allowed to rear their own children. Public nurseries and schools cared for the children from infancy and educated them in ways appropriate to the rank to which they belonged. Boys of noble families underwent a spartan discipline in plain and simple living and in the virtues of honor, justice, courage, modesty, clemency, religion and patriotism. They were kept busy and well-supervised, and their parents were allowed to see them only twice a year – in the presence of a professor. Children of business and manufacturing families were sent to work as apprentices at the age of 11. Girls' education was much like that of boys, with special care being taken to avoid the errors in education practised on English girls.

Gulliver next gives an account of his servants in Lilliput and of his way of living. Hundreds of people sewed and cooked for him and served his meals. Once he entertained the royal family, with Flimnap present and looking as sour as ever. Resolving to ignore Flimnap's attitude, Gulliver ate more than usual – to win the admiration of his guests and to do honor to his "dear country." But his appetite and vanity thus betrayed him to the enmity of the treasurer, who redoubled his efforts to having others present.

With laughable seriousness and urgency, Gulliver defends the wife of Flimnap against malicious gossip that she was having an affair with Gulliver. He said that their relationship was that of innocent friendship and that, like other ladies of the court, she never visited him without having others present.

Commentary

Chapter 6 breaks the story line as we have been following it. Now, we have Lilliput in some ways presented as a utopia (an ideal country) – a utopia in theory, that is. Gulliver's introductory remarks about the perfect proportions of all things in Lilliput – men, horses, trees, birds and buildings keeping the same relative sizes they do in England – denotes Swift's careful planning of the book, and also makes it an interesting story children can share with adults. (Gulliver's description of a young girl threading an invisible needle with invisible silk, for example, points up how the sight of these little people is sharpened to enable them to deal with their little world.) And Swift's remark about their long-flourishing learning is a joke at the expense of his lady friends: the Lilliputians write aslant from corner to corner of the page like no other people in the world — except ladies in England.

Swift is highly ironic in having Gulliver describe the excellent laws and customs as "very peculiar" and say that he would try to justify them "if they were not so directly contrary to those of my own dear country." Those of his own dear country would be much improved by *not* being contrary to those of Lilliput.

The student should note well Gulliver's confession of being ashamed at the emperor's rebuke over the fraud case. Gulliver's defence of the runaway servant-thief was ". . . only a breach of trust." The emperor thinks it scandalous to offer as a defence the very circumstance that made the crime worse. Swift intends to have us examine our values. This is the first occasion on which Gulliver himself shows any signs of doubting the values with which he has lived in England, of supposing that another people may have some improvements to offer on the way of life in "his dear country."

It is also important to note Gulliver's caution that he has been discussing the original constitutions in Lilliput and *not* the actual state of affairs. In practice, Lilliput is scandalously corrupt. English readers of the day could make the satiric transition: the English were proud of their "ideal" constitution, but they were aware of great corruptions in practice and of the corrosive effects of "party and faction" to which Swift alludes. At this point, Gulliver speaks of selecting officers of honor and trust by rope-dancing or by leaping and creeping as an "infamous practice." Formerly, he had no criticism of the practice, but only found it amusing. This is a step in his education to new values.

The student should carefully study the whole discussion on education and remember it especially when Gulliver discusses the education and character of the English nobility in Books III and IV. Gulliver's utopian nobles are rigorously disciplined and trained to hard and worthy virtues. Note also the interest in women's education. Swift, in his own life, showed a practical interest in women's education, which was almost nonexistent at the time. Daniel Defoe (who wrote *Robinson Crusoe*) and Joseph Addison (who helped write *The Spectator* papers) share with Gulliver the argument for educating women that "a wife should be always a reasonable and agreeable companion, because she cannot always be young."

In the matter of defending the honor of Flimnap's wife, Swift is again laughing at Walpole — first for his stinginess of mind and second for the gossip that his wife "was no better than she should be." Walpole was well-known for his indifference to his wife's flirtations. But the incident here is interesting also as showing how totally Gulliver has been "taken in" by his environment, how thoroughly assimilated he is into the little world surrounding him. Otherwise, how could he, with a straight face, defend the lady (under six inches tall) against so physically ridiculous a charge?

CHAPTER 7

Summary

Gulliver recorded his surprise at finding that what he had heard of courts and princes in other countries was true in Lilliput. A court intrigue against him, led by Flimnap and Bolgolam, had succeeded in bringing charges of treason and other capital crimes against him. He was impeached for treason for "maliciously, traitorously, and devilishly" making water within the precincts of the royal palace; for declining to annihilate Blefuscudian power after he had captured its fleet; for "aiding, abetting, and comforting" the ambassadors of Blefuscu; for preparing to travel to Blefuscu with "only verbal licence from his Imperial Majesty" and thereby to "aid, comfort, and abet the Emperor of Blefuscu, so late an enemy."

Flimnap and Bolgolam demanded "the most painful and ignominious death" for the "traitor." Against them, Gulliver's friend, Reldresal, urged that justice would be satisfied if *in his great mercy* the emperor would merely have Gulliver blinded, but Bolgolam held out for the death penalty, angrily arguing that "all true reasons of state" made the man-mountain's services to Lilliput the greatest reasons for his execution. Flimnap agreed, arguing that the state could not long support the financial drain of maintaining the man-mountain and that blinding him would, as in the case of blinded fowl, only make him eat the more. That the emperor and council, he said, were convinced of Gulliver's guilt was sufficient reason to condemn him "without the *formal proofs required by the strict letter of the law*." When the emperor decided in favor of blinding the "traitor," and of inflicting some other additional punishment, Reldresal suggested that Gulliver might be slowly starved to death. Disposing of his diminished carcass would then be less of a problem. In three days, said Gulliver's informant, Reldresal would arrive to read the articles of impeachment to Gulliver, and 20 surgeons would put out his eyes. Gulliver considered what he might do. He might stay to be tried. He might destroy the Lilliputian empire. But the remembrance of the favors he had received led him to flee to the court of Blefuscu, where he was royally welcomed.

Commentary

Swift is again concerned with the events surrounding the Treaty of Utrecht and the conduct of the Whigs after the death of Queen Anne. The secrecy of the court action against Gulliver mocks Walpole's aptly named Committee of Secrecy that brought charges of treason against Harley, Bolingbroke and other Tory leaders after the Queen's death. We may note that "only verbal licence" suggests the Tory contacts with French diplomats toward a peace treaty (1711-12) carried on without written authorization under the Great Seal.

Gulliver describes how the emperor's celebrated speeches on his own leniency and mercy always set the kingdom trembling because they always precede some inhuman punishment or savage executions. Thus, Swift satirically touches a horror of 1716, when an address of the House of Lords, praising the "endearing tenderness and clemency" of King George I, was closely followed by the executions of the Tory leaders of a 1715 rebellion. And, of course, the reader cannot miss the parallel irony of the emperor's decision to blind Gulliver in the name of mercy.

The proposal to blind Gulliver while he lies on the ground to receive into his eyeballs the arrows shot by 20 surgeons, exposes both the monstrous cruelty of the puny Lilliputians and their vanity. They expect this man-mountain, who could easily flick them out of existence, to submit meekly to their underhandedly-prepared and unjust sentence. Gulliver's combination of physical and moral superiority to these nasty little plotters shows an essential nobility of character. The *nice irony* of Gulliver on the ways of courts in this part of the story deserves a rereading: his simple, honest mind is unable to discover the *lenity and favor* of his sentence. If he had then "known the nature of princes and ministers," as he later came to know them, he should "with great alacrity and readiness have submitted to so easy a punishment." But he was hurried away "by the precipitancy of youth" to save his eyes and his life by fleeing the country. His flight seems to represent Bolingbroke's escape to France just as the Whigs were about to arrest him.

CHAPTER 8

Summary

Three days after landing in Blefuscu, Gulliver luckily came upon a boat which he supposed had been lost by some ship in a storm. With great effort and with much help from the Blefuscudians, he brought the boat to shore and fitted it out for his departure. Meanwhile, the emperor of Blefuscu was diplomatically fending off demands from Lilliput that the man-mountain be returned for punishment as a traitor. The emperor of Blefuscu privately proposed that Gulliver, in exchange for the emperor's "protection," remain in the Blefuscudian service. But Gulliver, wiser now than to put his trust in princes, made his own diplomatic excuses and perceived that the emperor and his ministers were glad to know that he would soon be gone.

Besides provisions for his journey, Gulliver took aboard his boat some of the small cattle and sheep of Blefuscu (intending to propagate them in England), 10,000 *sprugs* (Blefuscudian coins), and a full-length picture of the emperor. But the emperor took care not to allow Gulliver to depart with any Blefuscudians, even with their own consent and desire. Not long after sailing from the island, Gulliver was picked up by an English merchantman, whose captain, John Biddle, could not believe Gulliver's story until he saw the small cattle and other trophies from Blefuscu. On April 13, 1702, Gulliver arrived home in England. He earned considerable money by showing his little animals to people of quality and finally sold the cattle for 600 pounds. Since that time they have thrived and multiplied, and Gulliver hopes that they will prove a boon to the English wool industry by providing a finer wool than has ever yet been known to it. A combination of financial improvements allowed Gulliver to leave his wife in comfortable circumstances when he next sailed away.

Commentary

Just as Lilliput tried to have Gulliver returned for trial, the English Whig government sought to have France return English exiles. Along with the political allegory, Swift remembers to develop Gulliver's character. If the man-mountain had not experienced Lilliput, he would doubtless have accepted the Blefuscudian emperor's invitation; but Gulliver's education is progressing.

Gulliver returns to England as he came — in a ship. The little empires he has visited are thus reaffirmed to be part of the real world. And *verisimilitude* is strengthened because a curious reader might inquire after and find the little animals that are thriving in England. Gulliver's love of country is apparent in his concern for the improvement of its wool industry, a leading component of England's economy. His affectionate nature is seen in his tender visit with his family, and their parting with "tears on both sides."

SUMMARY OF BOOK I

Book I presents Gulliver's character as basically humane, simple, good-natured, patriotic and honest. He is the friend of man. His education progresses by experience. He is not bitter yet, but he is wary of princes at the end of the book. Swift represents Tory-Whig politics in a political allegory seen from the Tory point of view. In a larger meaning, the book views man in his smallness, both physical and moral. Lilliputian virtues are as puny as Lilliputian bodies. In the face of the universe, Swift would say, man is Lilliputian; but his ridiculous pride blinds him to his insignificance, his enormous vices and his paltry efforts at doing good.

From time to time, the reader has been given indications that Book I is written from a position in time *following* Book IV, as when Gulliver remarks, ". . . if I had then known the nature of princes and ministers, which I have since observed in many other courts. . . ." The point is important: Gulliver does not write like a man insane, nor like a misanthrope (man-hater), nor does he revise Book I to bring its mildness into conformity with the violence of Book IV.

Book II — A Voyage to Brobdingnag

CHAPTER 1

Summary

After two restless months in England, Gulliver again set sail, on June 20, 1702, aboard the *Adventure*, bound for Surat. Two great storms blew the ship off course, far to the east of the Molucca Islands, until the oldest seaman aboard did not know what part of the world lay around it. On June 16, 1703, uncharted land appeared. A party of men, including Gulliver, went ashore for water. Wandering alone on a hilltop, Gulliver suddenly saw his fellow sailors rowing desperately back towards the ship from a monster of a man who pursued on foot. Sharp, pointed rocks in the sea prevented the monster from reaching them, and they sailed away, leaving Gulliver behind. Gulliver hid in a field of corn whose stalks were 40 feet high, while seven monsters with enormous reaping hooks cut the corn closer and closer to Gulliver. In this difficulty he could not forbear thinking of the Lilliputians, whom he had put in a similar predicament, and he remembered the philosophers who had said that nothing is great or small except by comparison.

In fear of being trampled to death by these mountainous men, or of being cut to pieces by their reaping hooks, Gulliver decided to give himself up. One of the reapers picked him up cautiously, as one would a small dangerous animal, to examine him closely — 60 feet in the air. Though he grievously pinched Gulliver's sides, the reaper did not harm him but turned him over to his master, a farmer. Unable to imagine what the "little" creature was, this man decided that Gulliver seemed rational and took him home to his family. He placed the new curiosity upon the table set for dinner. Though the sound of their speech almost deafened Gulliver, they could barely hear his shouting and, of course, neither they nor he could make anything of the other's language. During the meal, the farmer's youngest boy, ten years old, picked the little stranger up by the legs and swung him in the air, a cat three times the size of an ox struck terror into him, and the baby snatched him up and put his head in its mouth. Gulliver's roar so frightened the baby that it had to be nursed into quiet. The nurse's breast, seen at close range by Gulliver's now microscopic eye, utterly revolted our traveller because of its giant size, its color, and its "spots, pimples, and freckles." He reflected that the skin of the fair women of England would probably look as marked and discolored if seen in a magnifying glass, and he remembered a Lilliputian who had told him of huge holes in his skin, though he was considered fair by English standards. He remembered, too, being unable to distinguish the facial characteristics of the tiny Lilliputians.

After lunch, the farmer's wife carried Gulliver to rest on a bed, 20 yards wide and eight yards from the floor, in a room 300 feet wide and over 200 feet high. Here, two rats attacked him. With his sword he killed one and slashed the other as it fled. He found the tail of the dead rat to be two yards long. When the farmer's wife returned, it was with great difficulty that he conveyed by signs to her that he labored under a great necessity to "discharge his natural functions." At last she set him free in the garden, and there, hidden between two sorrel leaves, he relieved himself.

Commentary

Again, Swift places his wonderland in an unmapped part of the world. No one can absolutely deny Gulliver's story, though the believer may now fill in another blank on his own map. Thus, early in Book II Gulliver announces that he will play the Lilliputian this time, among the men-mountains. Though he remembers the Lilliputians, he seems not to remember the relative ferocity of the roles he and they played; and so he terrifies himself with the popular untruth that men are "more savage and cruel in proportion to their bulk." In Book I Gulliver had not proved it true.

Despite having taken the place of the Lilliputians, he seems more ridiculous than they as he stumbles over a crust on the table and is surrounded by the hugeness of all things Brobdingnagian — the enormous cat; the dog (as large as four elephants); a baby so large that when it dropped Gulliver, the former man-mountain would have been killed had he not been saved from striking the floor.

In speaking of having to relieve himself, Gulliver returns to his scatological (excremental) frankness, as though he had not shown man poor enough and contemptible enough already. But he defends his attention to this painful scene because it is suited to "help a philosopher to enlarge his thoughts and imagination and apply them to the benefit of public as well as private life," which he declares is his sole purpose in presenting all his travels to the world.

CHAPTER 2

Summary

The farmer had a daughter (only 40 feet tall — small for her nine years) who took complete charge of Gulliver, dressing him, undressing him, sewing shirts for him of material coarser than sack-cloth, and washing him. She also taught him the language. The two quickly became fond of each other. To her, he was "Grildrig" (little man) and, to him, she was "Glumdalclitch" (little nurse). The neighbors flocked to view this curious human-shaped animal which, set upon a table, could speak their language. Following the advice of a miserly old visitor who had provoked Gulliver's laughter and had resented it, the master decided to expose his curiosity for money in the town on the next market day. Gulliver was indignant at the prospect of becoming a freak show, and Glumdalclitch feared that some harm might come to him from mishandling by thoughtless people. She dreaded that this new pet of hers would follow a parallel with a pet lamb which her parents had given her and then, when it was fattened, had sold to a butcher. Gulliver worried less than his nurse, for he hoped one day to recover his liberty. To console himself for the humiliation of becoming a spectacle, he reflected that under the same circumstances, the king of Great Britain would have fared exactly the same.

To market, then, Gulliver was carried in a box with a few holes to admit air, terribly shaken and discomposed by the motion of the giant horse. Twelve times that day he entertained the country bumpkins of Brobdingnag by answering questions, turning himself about, welcoming the audience, drinking to the health of the spectators, and flourishing his sword in a tavern. One small boy fired a hazelnut of pumpkin size at Gulliver's head, which would have been smashed had the aim been good. So successful was this showing that the farmer decided to repeat it on the next market day, and soon Gulliver was putting on a show daily except Wednesday, their sabbath. Two months after his arrival, Gulliver set out with his master and nurse on a tour of the cities of the kingdom. Glumdalclitch carried him on her lap in a box lined with soft cloth, to prevent injury from the jolts of the horse. In Lorbrulgrud (Pride of the Universe), capital city of the country, he was shown ten times a day to delighted crowds.

Commentary

Gulliver makes nothing of his humiliating position as the plaything of a little girl, the equal of a toy or doll; but his dignity as a man is erased despite his affection for Glumdalclitch. To her, he is a pet, not a person, the equal of a pet lamb she had lost. His humiliation will soon be greater, when he becomes a public curiosity men pay to see. So far as position is concerned, Swift has here stripped man of all reason for pride, but Gulliver will cling to his despite his circumstances. On the other hand, he reveals good human traits in his gratitude and love for Glumdalclitch (he might have chosen to sulk and resent her care).

Thus far, the moral character of the Brobdingnagians takes only the pattern of humanity. Some are kindly, thoughtful, loving, like Glumdalclitch and her mother and some are greedy, like the farmer and his miser friend. Boys are thoughtless, mischievous and constitutionally cruel, like the hazelnut thrower or Glumdalclitch's brother. Later, the reader will have reason to see that Swift intends to fashion a more definite moral pattern in the giants of his second book.

CHAPTER 3

Summary

This rigorous schedule of showings destroyed Gulliver's health. He grew thin as a skeleton. His master, thinking he would soon die, snatched at the chance to sell him to the queen, who found this creature so amusing that she willingly paid a great price for him. The king, however, was puzzled and suspicious of Gulliver. He had three great scholars examine the strange little thing and give their opinion of its nature. One decided it was an embryo, a solution rejected by the other two because all of its limbs were well formed and its beard proved it had been living for several years. At last, they came to the conclusion that he was a "relplum scalcath," a freak of nature. This, Gulliver took to be a solution consistent with the findings of the modern philosophical mind.

The king then ordered that Gulliver receive the best of care, with Glumdalclitch in charge. She, too, was to live at court and be given a governess for her education, a personal maid and two servants. At the queen's command, a box was made for Gulliver, according to specifications furnished by him and Glumdalclitch: 16 feet square and 12 high, with three windows, a door, two closets and a lock to prevent rats from entering.

The queen grew so fond of Gulliver that she could scarcely dine without him. On Wednesdays (their sabbath) he dined with the entire royal family, at which time the king elicited from his tiny guest an account of the laws, religion and education in Europe. Gulliver's earnest account of affairs in England provoked the king to hearty laughter and the teasing question, "Are you a Whig or a Tory?" He reflected on "how contemptible a thing was human grandeur, which could be mimicked by such diminutive insects."

As time went on, Gulliver grew so used to these gargantuan people that the thought of tiny Englishmen strutting around in their pride and finery tempted him to laugh also. His environment made him shrink in his own imagination until he thought of himself as having dwindled down to a fraction of his size. Everything in Brobdingnag conspired against his self-esteem. The queen's dwarf, whose diminutive height (only 30 feet) made him glory in finding someone smaller than himself, teased and bullied Gulliver. Once, he threw his rival into a bowl of cream and, once, he wedged Gulliver into the hollow of a marrow-bone. The dwarf was punished and finally sold as being too dangerous to have around Gulliver. One morning at breakfast, attacked by 20 giant wasps, Gulliver killed four of them and routed the rest with his sword. The stings of his slain enemies he brought home to England, where three of them were displayed in Gresham College.

Commentary

Gulliver has become a slave, a *thing* that is bought and sold to amuse his masters, and his humiliation deepens as he becomes a specimen, a subject of laboratory examination. But Swift is here more interested in ridiculing the scholars and through them the modern philosophers of his time than he is in Gulliver's plight. The scholars' narrowness prevents their imagining an environment in which a creature like Gulliver might be capable of surviving, and their final determination, which merely pins a meaningless term to Gulliver, is Swift's jeer at modern philosophy's new ways of disguising old ignorance — "to the unspeakable advancement of human knowledge." The Brobdingnagians, however, are not all fools. The king has a better understanding than his scholars, as he shows by questioning the farmer, Gulliver and Glumdalclitch, and beginning to believe their story.

The Brobdingnagian king continues to show a steady intelligence. He is aware that human (i.e., Brobdingnagian) grandeur is contemptible when it can be imitated by such "insects" as Gulliver. He reveals a knowledge of his own people and their character — and Swift thus contrives to pass it on to us — when he imagines that, like the Brobdingnagians, the tiny English "have their titles and distinctions of honour; they contrive little nests and burrows, that they call houses and cities; they make a figure in dress and equipage; they love, they fight, they dispute, they cheat, they betray." The "insect," Gulliver, burns with humiliation at the king's contempt. Under these circumstances, Gulliver is amusing when he bristles with indignation at hearing his noble country, "the mistress of arts and arms, the scourge of France, the arbitress of Europe, the seat of virtue, piety, honour, and truth, the pride and envy of the world," belittled. How hollow his boasting little "patriotism" sounds in the presence of the giant king and his court! How Lilliputian!

For some time the story has read as though Swift's organizing principle is to exploit all imaginable ways of belittling human self-esteem. To the reader who is willing to recognize the truth of Swift's analysis, the author is succeeding very well. The Brobdingnagian king, like Gulliver himself, peers through the outer surfaces into the realities beneath.

Gresham College, the seat of the Royal Society in London for promoting scientific knowledge, becomes another link of the known world with the unknown parts Gulliver describes, because it now houses the stings from some Brobdingnagian wasps. The student may, at his next visit to the Royal Society, examine the one-and-one-half-inch stings of Gulliver's wasps.

CHAPTER 4

Summary

Gulliver then described the Brobdingnagian country and offered to assist geographers in correcting their maps. The king's dominion extended to 6,000 miles in length and from three to five in breadth. How wrong were the geographers of Europe in thinking that nothing lay between California and Japan! Naturally, something must counterpoise Tartary on the globe; it was this vast tract of land on the northwest part of America. The land was a peninsula cut off from the rest of the continent by impassable mountains 30 miles high and topped with active volcanoes. On three sides the land was surrounded by the ocean, but lacked any seaport because of pointed rocks and rough seas. Since all fish from the ocean were of European size, the natives did not consider them worth catching; but in their own rivers they found excellent fish of a useful size.

The country had 51 cities, 100 walled towns and numerous villages. Lorbrulgrud, the capital city where Gulliver lived, had about 600,000 people. The king's palace was unusual because it was a compound of several buildings about seven miles in circumference. Riding about town in a coach the size of Westminster Hall, Gulliver saw people who filled him with revulsion because the diseased parts of their bodies were to his eyes greatly magnified — a woman with a monstrous breast-cancer, a man with a tumor "the size of two wool-packs." But most hateful of all was the sight of huge lice rooting like swine with their snouts in the great coarse skins of living people. Gulliver was disappointed to find the height of their chief temple only 3,000 feet, relatively low in proportion to the size of the people. At the base of the temple, Glumdalclitch found a finger fallen from one of the statues. It was four feet and one inch long. The traveller observed how typically childish Glumdalclitch was to put it in a collection of such trinkets.

The king's kitchen was 600 feet high, though the oven was not as wide as the cupola at St. Paul's. Gulliver interrupted himself at this point for fear of censorship by his readers, who might suppose Gulliver exaggerated wonders like other travellers. The Brobdingnagians, indeed, should they chance upon his book, would have reason to complain that he had diminished their country in his telling.

Commentary

Swift prudently supplies Brobdingnag with no harbors, else readers might wonder why none of the giants' giant ships are ever encountered on the seas. Everything in the country is on a scale to paralyze imagination: mountains 30 miles high, a city 54 miles long and 45 broad yet peopled with such out-sized citizens that there are only 600,000 of them.

CHAPTER 5

Summary

Because of his size, Gulliver suffered some peculiar adventures in Brobdingnag. One day, after Glumdalclitch left him under some dwarf apple trees, the queen's dwarf joined him. Gulliver alluded to the likeness in names of the dwarf and the trees. Provoked, the dwarf shook the tree, and apples the size of barrels came tumbling down around Gulliver's head. Another day, left alone in a field, he found himself unprotected from a storm of hailstones 1,800 times the size of England's hail. Once, a spaniel took him in its mouth and carried him, luckily unharmed, to its master. All these incidents Gulliver suffered in great embarrassment, danger and pain.

The maids of honor often invited Glumdalclitch and Gulliver to their apartments. Here, again, Gulliver experienced disgust with the ugliness of the body seen too closely and too well. He complained of an offensive odor coming from their skins, yet he supposed that these same people were no more offensive to their lovers than were similar people in England to theirs. He remembered being told by a Lilliputian friend of an offensive smell coming from Gulliver's body. Nothing natural, however, was as offensive as the Brobdingnagians' perfume, which immediately made him faint. Gulliver resented the way the maids treated him as being of no consequence. They would undress themselves in his presence, but he found the sight no tempting one. He saw moles on them as broad as large plates, and the hairs hanging from the moles looked like pack-thread. In front of him they would relieve themselves of over 120 gallons of urine. He especially begged Glumdalclitch to keep him away from one pleasant, frolicksome lass of 16 who liked to set Gulliver astride one of her nipples and play other tricks Gulliver excused himself from describing. One day, Gulliver witnessed the execution of a murderer. It was grotesque to see a forty-foot blade cut off the head and cause blood to spout into the air higher than the fountain at Versailles (over 70 feet).

Because Gulliver was cheered by mention of the sea, the queen offered to have a boat built for him to sail. With it she supplied a wooden trough 300 feet long, 50 feet wide, and eight feet deep, which, when filled with water, was ample to allow Gulliver to exhibit his great skill in rowing and sailing for the entertainment of the ladies of the court. Sometimes they raised a gale for him with their fans.

Gulliver recalled his most dangerous adventure. Once, a monkey snatched him up and leaped out a window to the roof. Apparently, the monkey took Grildrig for a young one of its own kind, for there, 900 feet above the ground, it began cramming nasty stuff from its own mouth into that of Gulliver's, who was nauseated nearly to death. Gulliver was rescued, the monkey was killed, but once again Gulliver was the target of the court's jokes. Even the king teasingly asked him about the details of his experience; Gulliver swaggered about what he would have done *if* he had thought of using his sword against the monkey, but he subsided, remarking the futility of anyone's trying to do himself honor among those entirely beyond comparison with him. Yet he reported having seen insignificant people in England presume to place themselves on a level with the greatest people in the kingdom. Sometimes Gulliver made himself ridiculous entirely on his own initiative, as happened one day when he desired to exhibit his physical prowess. Attempting to leap over cow dung, he landed short — in the nasty stuff up to his knees.

Commentary

That the hailstones are 1,800 times the size of English hailstones reminds us that Swift still keeps proportions in the sizes of objects. The Lilliputians reckoned the bulk of Gulliver's body to be 1,728 times that of their own. The Brobdingnagian hailstones show roughly the same proportion to "ours" in bulk. In Lilliput, the proportions in heights were one to 12 (six inches to seventy-two); in Brobdingnag they are roughly similar (something over ten to one). An English church spire, corresponding to the spire Gulliver reports, would be nearly 300 feet high. Salisbury Cathedral has the tallest spire in England, 404 feet high; but Gulliver seems to be reaching hard to find *some* superiority in *some*thing English (for the honor of his dear country) when he refuses to be impressed with a temple towering *only* 3,000 feet into the air. His vanity dies hard, or not at all.

Swift incessantly hammers against man's — and woman's — vanity and pride. Here and elsewhere (especially in some of his poems), he undermines romantic notions of love and romantic notions of self-glorification. Doubtless, the court maids whose basic animality is here exposed, were, in their own eyes and in those of their lovers, beautiful, young and attractive. Swift loves to scrape off the cosmetics. He who wishes may read the meaning.

Swift shows that Gulliver (man) needs no external force, no monkey, to make him ridiculous. He is by nature ridiculous, and his vanity will not fail to supply onlookers with enough to laugh about.

CHAPTER 6

Summary

Gulliver tried to please the king and queen by employing his mechanical genius in making such things as a comb from the stumps of the king's beard and "cane" chairs from the combings of the queen's hair. Of the same material he made a purse for Glumdalclitch. He devised a system for playing Glumdalclitch's spinet by running up and down the great keyboard, banging keys with two large poles. But he found it a great disadvantage not to be able to reach both bass and treble keys at one time.

At this point, the king questioned Gulliver about his country and learned in detail about the climate, the soil, the institutions and the history of England. Gulliver spoke of the House of Peers, representing the noblest, most ancient and wealthy families. Their valor, fidelity and skill in arms and arts qualified them to share in the legislature. With them were associated men of holy living, selected by the prince and his wisest counsellors. The other part of parliament was the House of Commons, consisting of gentlemen freely selected by the people. Over the courts presided venerable judges to mediate disputes, punish vice, and protect innocence; and the various other officers of government and the armed forces shone with the highest virtues proper to their stations.

The king listened, took notes, but said nothing until Gulliver was finished. Then the king indicated many doubts, raising objections on every point. He asked what educational preparation was received by lords, how they were selected, what the motives for advancement were, whether the holy lords were selected for their religious knowledge and sanctity, how a commoner was elected if it was so expensive to be elected, and what the reward was for buying this office. Next he attacked the courts of justice, asking how well qualified the judges were, what reward they received for their decisions, and whether they were ever admitted to the lower senate. Then, calculating the expenses ("issues") of the government for one year, the king found them more than twice the amount of tax income. He said that the English must be a quarrelsome people or must be surrounded by troublesome neighbors, and their generals must be richer than their kings. He was puzzled at the idea of a standing army in peacetime.

The king saw through the corruption of English life and institutions — that the nobles were effete and vicious, the parliament a collection of ignorant, corrupt, and idle men; the laws explained and interpreted by those who profited by perverting, confounding, and eluding them. The history of England was a record, he said, of conspiracies, rebellions, murders, massacres, revolutions. In short, despite hints that the establishment might originally have been acceptable, Gulliver's people were "the most pernicious race of little odious vermin that nature ever suffered to crawl upon the surface of the earth."

Commentary

Gulliver's account of England, like his account of Lilliput, first presents the country as a utopia. Prior to beginning his account, Gulliver makes clear his patriotic enthusiasm: ". . . how often I then wished for the tongue of a Demosthenes or Cicero . . . to celebrate the praise of my own dear native country in a style equal to its merits and felicity." Gulliver wishes to praise, not describe (because of his pride in England).

And any account from a man who wants to speak like one of the world's two greatest orators is bound to be more oratorical than honest.

Swift sounds a solid Tory line and opposes such Whig policies as financing wars by running up a national debt and keeping a standing army in peacetime. The Tories consistently charged that the Whig government was wasting the national wealth in mismanagement and corruption (the expenses of the government were twice as large as the income). And the remark about generals richer than kings would remind English readers of the Whig general, Marlborough, who made a very good thing financially of war — or so the Tories maintained. He was scandalously well-rewarded by his adoring nation and charged by the Tories with prolonging the War of the Spanish Succession in order to continue grafting on the grand scale with army money.

Gulliver's effort has backfired. He had hoped to impress the king with England's might, grandeur, and greatness. Instead, he receives a most crushing and humiliating verdict, which reduces the English to "the most pernicious race of little odious vermin."

For some time now, Gulliver has been used by Swift as a satiric device known as the *obtuse* or *self-defeating mask*, a character invented by the satirist to defend the "wrong" side of a question and, without realizing what he is doing, to deliver the "wrong" side to destruction. Thus, the Tory Swift has made Gulliver defend — and surrender — Whig positions. Thus, the Swift who wishes to destroy men's false pride in their national institutions has entrusted Gulliver with defending those institutions, with the results we have seen.

CHAPTER 7

Summary

Gulliver regretted the results of the king's sharp inquiries. Indeed, only love of truth could hinder him from concealing this part of the story. He had done his best, artfully eluding many of the king's questions and even considerably improving on the strict truth about England, wishing to hide the faults and magnify the virtues of his political mother. But his endeavor had "unfortunately failed of success."

To please the king, Gulliver told him of gunpowder, of its terrible power, and its uses. It destroys whole armies, sinks ships with their crews of a thousand men each, batters down walls, and divides hundreds of bodies with one shot. Gulliver's offer to teach the king how to make it was met with complete horror by the king, who considered the inventor to be an enemy of mankind, an evil genius, and he was amazed that such an insect as Gulliver could entertain such inhuman ideas. As for himself, the king would rather lose half the kingdom than to share such a secret; and he commanded Gulliver as he valued his life not to mention it to anyone.

Stung by his humiliation, Gulliver delivered a speech in which he points out some European superiorities to the Brobdingnagians. The king abominated (Gulliver says "professed to abominate" as though he suspected the honesty of the king) mystery, refinement, and intrigue, those usual methods of operating in courts. He and his people reject "all abstractions and transcendentals." The laws were limited to 22 words, and any person could interpret them in one reading. To write a commentary on a law was a capital offence. Though they had been printing as long as the Chinese, their libraries were small. The largest, the king's, had only 1,000 volumes. In writing, "their style is clear, masculine, and smooth, but not florid;" for they aimed at conciseness and simple, unornamented statement.

Gulliver described the contents of a book of morality and devotion much like those of Europe. After dwelling on man's contemptible and helpless conditions, it lamented how nature "was degenerated in these later declining ages of the world," that it could now produce only "small abortive births" in contrast with the giants it had formerly produced. That the giants make these complaints against nature made Gulliver conclude that the same complaints in European writers were probably as ill-grounded as they were in Brobdingnag.

The Brobdingnagian army was a citizen militia of 176,000 men who were, Gulliver grudgingly admitted, well-disciplined and well-trained. Once he saw 6,000 of the cavalry draw their swords at command and brandish them in the air.

Commentary

Gulliver shows some inkling of why he failed: he was defending a bad cause, one whose faults *needed* to be glossed over and whose virtues magnified. But he still remains the obtuse mask, for he is not yet disillusioned. He blames his failure mostly on the "prejudices and narrowness of thinking" which operate in the giant king because of his isolation from the great world, but from which "we and the politer countries of Europe are wholly exempted." And Gulliver, to emphasize his own failure to learn from his experience, is now about to throw another boomerang that will return to injure him.

In a passage of splendid irony Swift comments on the king's reaction to the gunpowder proposal. Gulliver introduced the incident as showing "the miserable efforts of a *confined education*." And now, "A strange effect of *narrow principles* and *short* views!" he exclaims. It is really Gulliver — and we — who have the narrow principles and short views as well as the confined education. In a most Europe-damning sentence Gulliver speaks of the "nice, unnecessary scruple" which we in Europe cannot even conceive of, by which the prince passes up a chance to become a complete tyrant over his people. Far from *having* the scruple, Europeans cannot even master the *idea* of it. The obtuse mask is operating here. Gulliver is sure that this episode will cause a sharp drop in the regard English readers may have developed for the king of Brobdingnag. Observe, too, how Gulliver here reverses the role he played in Lilliput, where he refused to reduce the brave and free Blefuscudians to slavery. In each case it is the giant whose moral virtue matches his relative size.

Brobdingnag has its turn to be utopia. Here, things appear as they should be. The Brobdingnagian king (while Gulliver despises him) speaks for Swift, of honest, simple arrangements in government, with an absence of intrigue. If a man "can make two ears of corn or two blades of grass grow where one grew before," the king remarks, he is worth all politicians put together. Swift would have laws plain and so simple in meaning that no lawyers or interpreters need exist. He was impatient of philosophical jargon and arty conversation, and he admired what was practical and of profit to humanity. He suggests that a good library might better contain a modest number of serviceable, much-used volumes than a vast collection of unread books.

When puny Gulliver, after the moral shrinking he has just endured, assumes a tone of contempt and superiority toward the superior Brobdingnagians, he earns our contempt — as Swift would wish, for in despising Gulliver's faults, we despise our own.

Upon seeing the Brobdingnagian militia flash their swords, Gulliver describes it:

> Imagination can figure nothing so grand, so surprising, and so astonishing . . . as if ten thousand flashes of lightning were darting at the same time from every quarter of the sky.

Gulliver puts us in mind of the admiration his single scimitar excited in the Lilliputians. The giants' army is not a Whig-type standing army of professionals, but, as it would be in a Tory utopia, a citizens' militia. Gulliver reports that, after a civil war, years ago, the Brobdingnagians had disbanded the opposing armies and set up the militia.

CHAPTER 8

Summary
The king entertained ideas of capturing a stray ship in order to mate Gulliver and cultivate this tiny race. Gulliver himself would rather have died than beget children fated to be kept in cages and treated as curiosities. He was aware that his kind treatment at court nevertheless left him in a condition lacking all human dignity, and he longed for liberty and his own people. After being in this land for two years, Gulliver, with Glumdalclitch, decided to join the king and queen on a journey to the coast. Near the sea, a page was entrusted with Gulliver to take him out for some fresh air. Thinking his small charge asleep, the

page wandered off in search of birds' eggs among the rocks. Gulliver awoke to find his box being carried out to sea by an eagle. After four hours the eagle dropped the box into the sea, and Gulliver was eventually picked up by an English ship. He sailed safely home to his wife and daughter in England, where he told and retold his tale and showed the proofs of Brobdingnag's reality he had managed to salvage from his box. Accustomed to the Brobdingnagian environment, he amazed people by shouting when he wished to speak and by warning them out of his way as though he might step on them. He stooped to avoid striking the top of the doorframe of his house, and his wife seemed to have shrunk to nearly nothing. He bent down lower than her knees to let her kiss him. It was some time before he persuaded those about him that he was indeed of sound mind.

Commentary

Swift is at pains to emphasize the psychological effect on Gulliver living among the giants. He has lost his mental bearings, as he did among the Lilliputians, where he failed to realize he had no need to defend the honor of Flimnap's wife. Now he supposed that he would step on men of his own size unless they get out of his path.

Again, Gulliver comes home by sea in an English ship, making Brobdingnag part of the real world and emphasizing that what happens in Brobdingnag happens to men in another country of the world. What they do is possible for Englishmen to do.

SUMMARY OF BOOK II

Gulliver in Brobdingnag becomes a Lilliputian morally as well as physically. Many details of the book remind the reader of the Lilliputian experience. But, since we have become identified with Gulliver, we also become Lilliputians. At the same time, we are given a contrasting view of man as the giant he may be if he wills it.

The Brobdingnagian king has a moral nobility to match his physical size. He is a big man. He is humble, always aware of man's limitations. He is a ruler attentive to the needs and the nature of his people. He is wise and thoughtful: Gulliver cannot impose on him. He is humane and lacks wicked ambition, as shows clearly in his indignant refusal of gunpowder and its potential increase of his own power. The reader should not be surprised, therefore, that with this model man as king, Brobdingnag has an organization, institutions, and laws that are also models for human imitation. The Brobdingnagians are not all saints: avarice and cruelty exist among them, and one was executed for murder. But the best Brobdingnagians, those in a position to represent their people, the king and queen, show no serious faults. And their constitution, unlike that of Lilliput, has *not* suffered corruption. Brobdingnag remains a utopia in spite of the presence of fallen human nature with its weaknesses, evils, and tendency to pull down good institutions.

Book III — A Voyage to Laputa, Balnibarbi, Lugg-nagg, Glubbdubdrib and Japan

CHAPTER 1

Summary
In 1706, after being made captain of a trading sloop off the Indo-China coast, Gulliver was blown off course in a storm and lost his ship to two pirates. His crew was divided equally between the two pirate ships. His sloop was manned by pirates and he, himself, narrowly escaped death from the malignity of a Dutch pirate who seemed to stand high among his fellows. He set adrift in a small canoe with eight days' provisions (generously and secretly doubled from four by the kindness of the Japanese pirate captain).

Sighting several islands, Gulliver sailed from one to another until, on the fifth day, he arrived at the last of them, an apparently deserted one, where he spent a night in a dry cave. His mind was troubled, thinking that on this solitary island he should arrive at his miserable end. The next day an opaque body suddenly cut off the sun's light. To his astonishment he discovered that it was an island flying about two miles high in the air. The bottom surface looked flat, smooth, and shining from the reflection of the sea. Viewing it with his pocket glass, he could see a vast number of people moving up and down on its sides, which seemed to be sloping. Startled at seeing an island floating in the sky, Gulliver was, nevertheless, thrilled at seeing people. The island seemed to rise and sink and move forward at the men's will. When it came nearer, he could see several galleries and stairs connecting each level. In the lowest part he could see people fishing. By shouting and waving, Gulliver attracted the attention of these flying islanders. The island descended to about 100 yards above the spot where Gulliver stood. A seat was let down to him on chains, and he was pulled up.

Commentary
Swift makes the heathen Japanese captain appear humane, kind, civilized by contrast with the supposedly christian Dutchman. Swift several times permits a bias against the Dutch to appear, even though they were the allies of England in the War of the Spanish Succession, which was raging in 1707 when the pirate episode supposedly occurred. The Tories had several grudges against the Dutch — for having a republic (anti-monarchy), for having religious toleration (anti-Established Church), and for being the most successful commercial people in Europe and, hence, a natural rival for seafaring Britain. Politically, the Tories argued that in the War of the Spanish Succession England suffered and won battles on the European continent but the Dutch took most of the profit. (See Swift's pamphlets, *The Conduct of the Allies and*

of the Late Ministry in Beginning and Carrying on the Present War and *Some Remarks on the Barrier Treaty*.

Swift's first scientific wonder is a flying machine, a gigantic one. Men had dreamed of flying machines from at least the time of the Greeks. Swift's is constructed in science-fiction style, on a scientific principle, thatof the attraction and repulsion of magnetic objects.

CHAPTER 2

Summary

Upon ascending, Gulliver was greeted by a large crowd of people. They all looked exactly alike. Their heads were inclined either to the left or to the right, one eye was turned inward and the other looked directly at the zenith. Their clothes bore designs of suns, moons and stars, with figures of fiddles, flutes, harps, trumpets, guitars, harpsichords, and many unknown instruments. Then he saw something amazing. Servants carried short sticks to which were attached blown bladders containing dried peas or small pebbles. With these the servants would now and then flap the mouths or ears of people nearby. Gulliver learned that these people were absorbed in such intense thought that they had to be aroused whenever they had occasion to speak or listen. Sometimes by flapping a man's eyes the servant would save him from stumbling over an object or even a precipice.

Gulliver was taken to the royal palace at the top of the island, but several times along the way his escorts forgot what they were doing and had to be reminded by their flappers, who would tap their brains to stir their memories. Oddly, the king's throne room was filled with globes, spheres and all kinds of mathematical instruments. The king paid no attention to Gulliver's entrance, but remained absorbed for over an hour in a problem. When the king addressed Gulliver, a flapper immediately struck Gulliver's right ear, but the newcomer indicated that he needed no such help — which gave the islanders a low opinion of his mentality. Despite Gulliver's knowledge of languages, he could not communicate with the king until, with his usual facility in strange tongues, Gulliver had taken a few days to master that of the island.

On Laputa, Gulliver was fitted with clothes in a most unusual way. The tailor took his altitude with a quadrant and then with rulers and compassses made the dimensions and outlines of his body. After seven days the clothes arrived, poorly made and out of shape because of an error in calculation. At 11 o'clock of his second day on the island, Gulliver's ears were deafened by crashing music, performed by the entire court for three hours without intermission. Each person played his own instrument to accompany the music of the spheres which, Gulliver learned, was audible on certain occasions. Because of this people's fondness for mathematics, Gulliver's own knowledge of the science greatly helped his mastering of the Laputan language. All the ideas of the Laputans revolved around lines and figures. Everything was designed in geometrical terms, and the standard of good with them was mathematical or musical: a beautiful woman they would describe by reference to rhombs, circles, parallelograms, or other geometrical figures, or in terms of music. But alas, their houses were badly built, with the walls leaning towards each other and with never a right angle in any apartment, for the Laputans despised practical geometry as vulgar and mechanic! Their very brilliance in mathematical theory made them unable to direct the operations of their workmen. They were great bumblers in all the affairs of practical life. They were poor reasoners and yet great arguers. They had no imagination and even lacked the words to express any thoughts outside the sciences of mathematics and music.

These people also pursued astronomy, though it caused them trouble and fear. They dreaded changes in the celestial bodies that would destroy earth. The sun might swallow up the earth, they thought, or a comet's tail burn it up. The last comet narrowly missed brushing the globe, and the next, 30 years later, would probably destroy the world. If the earth should move a certain degree towards the sun, they said, it would be destroyed. They also worried that the sun would soon burn itself up, to the complete destruction of the earth and of all the planets. Because of these fears, the people never slept peacefully nor enjoyed the pleasures of life.

About this time, the Laputan king re-emphasized his concerns and his total indifference to practical matters.. He questioned Gulliver on the state of mathematics in England but showed no interest whatever in English religion, government, laws, history, or manners. How different he was from the Brobdingnagian king, who showed the greatest interest in such practical subjects and the deepest understanding not only of what was said but of what was not. The frequent need of the Laputan king to be brought to attention by a flapper even during the conversation deepened the contrast.

The women of the island, vivacious, but bored, were very fond of strangers who came to court from the continent below. Their husbands were so absorbed in mathematical problems that, unless the flapper was near, they never noticed their wives enjoying the company of their lovers from below. Wives and daughters, though treated magnificently, longed to leave the floating island and see the world below. This they could not do without permission from the king, who gave it reluctantly because once women went below they could scarcely be brought back again. Once the prime minister's wife went below on a visit and some months later was discovered living in rags with an old deformed footman. Brought back unwillingly to the island, she soon escaped again, taking all her jewels. The jewels she gave to the footman, but she disappeared entirely..This story, Gulliver observed, might sound like a European or an English story rather than one of an obscure country.

Commentary

Swift combines his inclinations for mere fun with his talent for satire when he has Gulliver mock the etymologists by his conjectures about the origin of the island's name, *Laputa*. In sum: he 1) gives up the problem by submitting it "to the judicious reader;" and 2) misses the most likely origin in the words *la puta* (Spanish, "the whore"). Lilliput might therefore suggest "little whore."

Swift is having a hilarious time with one of his favorite targets, the eccentricities and impracticalities of those devoted to pure science. Swift was always averse to abstract speculation (he received his A.B. *speciali gratia* — by special favor — of Trinity College, Dublin, because he would not apply himself to the required philosophy). Swift says nothing here about applied science. Nor does he seem to realize that the flying island is a most magnificent achievement in applied science. He is also satirizing a court filled with frenzied devotees of music, who are as cracked as the devotees of pure mathematics. Since George I of England strongly patronized music (and in a smaller way, science also), the Laputan king must be considered a figure of George.

Sir Isaac Newton's studies of the motions of heavenly bodies suggested that after many ages the earth might be swallowed up by the sun. Halley's comet inspired terror on earth in 1682, and some scientists, including Halley himself, had speculated that the earth might be struck and reduced to its original chaos. Swift's ridicule is not aimed at the predictions, but at people who waste time worrying over possible cosmic calamities over which man can have no control and in which he would quickly perish. He does aim at scientists whose speculations lead them and others to such fears.

With regard to the story of the Laputan prime minister's wife, there is little doubt about the specific subject of this satirical thrust. To Englishmen, *prime minister* meant Robert Walpole, who lacked the title, indeed, but was prime minister in fact. Walpole's son, the famous writer, Horace Walpole, was sure that Swift here intended another cut at his father.

CHAPTER 3

Summary

The flying island was a perfectly circular piece of adamant, its diameter about four miles and a half, its thickness 300 yards. It contained 10,000 acres. Its movement was controlled by a magnetic lodestone about six yards in length and three yards thick, sustained by a strong adamant axle and so perfectly poised that any hand could move it. When (at the king's command) the attracting end of the magnet was tilted towards the earth, the island was pulled downward; tilting the repelling end downward drove the island up again.

Because the Laputans had perfected telescopes far beyond

Europe's best, their astronomy had far surpassed that of Europe. They knew three times as many fixed stars as European astronomers. They had discovered two satellites about Mars, revolving from the center of the planet exactly three and five of its diameters, the first in ten hours and the second in twenty-one.

The king of Laputa was prevented from being an absolute tyrant because his ministers owned estates on the mainland below and they refused to join with the king to subject the country entirely to his will. In case of rebellion, the king used the island to cut off rain and sun from the rebellious parts of the mainland, and he could throw down stones from above. As a last resort, he could crush everything below by lowering the island to the ground. This maneuver he rarely used, for the ministers opposed the destruction of their estates and there was also danger of damaging the island on tall rocks, spires, or in fires. About three years before Gulliver's arrival, the monarchy nearly suffered destruction from a revolt in Lindalino, second greatest city in the kingdom.

Commentary

Swift (through Gulliver) gives a long and particular "philosophical account" of the structure and operation of the great lodestone. He is mocking, by imitation, the Royal Society's learned papers. (For a knowing study of the scientific bases and implications of Book III, see "The Scientific Background of Swift's Voyage to Laputa" in Marjorie H. Nicolson's *Science and Imagination*, pages 110-154.)

The astronomer, Charles P. Olivier, has called Swift's prophecy about the satellites of Mars and the main facts about their orbits "the most astonishing 'prophecy' of the past thousand years as to whose full authenticity there is no shadow of doubt." The prediction came a century before a telescope existed that could possibly reveal them, and a century and a half before the satellites were discovered (1877). Thus, Swift's satiric mockery has been undermined by the facts discovered since his time: his satire has backfired here.

Laputa's manner of government, which has communication with the mainland only by packthreads by which citizens may send up their petitions, suggests the absentee type of government from which Ireland suffered in the eighteenth century. Not only were its small landlords far removed from London, but worse, the controlling power of Irish government lay in distant London. In both cases, the country was miserable through being subject to a government far above its head, like the flying island, a government cut off from the interests of the people governed and (unlike the royal Brobdingnagian) totally ignorant of the situation of its people. Only the ministers' partial identifications of interests with those of the lower classes saved the country from perfect tyranny and destruction.

Lindalino is Dublin, and the revolt figuratively represents the uproar over Wood's coinage that produced Swift's *The Drapier's Letters* (1724). Swift roused opposition to an English project to flood Ireland with a large issue of copper coins which, Swift argued, would drive out whatever good money still remained in the island. Swift ridiculed William Wood, author of the plan, as well as the plan itself and the manner of Wood's obtaining his patent for the project — by bribing the Duchess of Kendal (the Lilliputian king's cushion which saved Flimnap in Book I). The four large towers in Gulliver's allegory seem to represent four churches, the most important and dangerous of which would be Swift's own St. Patrick's. The large quantity of combustible fuel would be pamphlets like *The Drapier's Letters* that set the Irish afire to refuse the coinage. The overshadowing island that deprives the city of sun and rain suggests English legal deprivations of Ireland's *natural* advantages — of trade and manufacture. It also suggests English interests and the English monarchical dominance over Ireland, both of which are in danger because of the accentuated conflict here with the interests of the subjected country. The towers thus represent the national interests of Ireland inviting a showdown, a head-on collision with the national interests of England. The student will profit from reading more about this very interesting struggle in a valuable book, *The Drapier's Letters*, edited by Herbert Davis (1935).

Gulliver's last paragraph in Chapter 3 reminded readers how George I quickly secured repeal of a provision of the 1701 Act of Settlement which required parliament's permission for the king to leave the country. George's favorite mistresses and other principal interests were in Germany, to which he frequently went for long visits, leaving the cabinet, usually Walpole and his Whigs, to manage the affairs of England.

Note how Gulliver's position in Laputa differs from those he filled in the first two books. Here, he takes no part in the activities of his environment. He merely writes reports on Laputa. The cause of the change seems to be in the absent-minded character of the Laputans, who are simply *not there* as people and personalities. The result is a lessening of movement, action and interest in the story. Gulliver himself, in the following chapter, makes the point that he was so thoroughly ignored that (like the wives and daughters in Laputa) he was soon glad to leave the island.

CHAPTER 4

Summary

Because Gulliver felt completely neglected by the people of Laputa, he decided to leave the island after two months. He received permission to leave through the influence of a great lord who, though he was accorded respect at court only because he was closely related to the king, was universally thought most ignorant and stupid. He was in many ways gifted, a man of honor and integrity, and had served the kingdom well. But he was a failure in mathematics and music. He paid attention to what was said to him, and used flappers only for ceremonial occasions.

Gulliver descended to Balnibarbi, the mainland, and to its capital city, Lagado. Introduced by a letter from the king's great relative, Gulliver was received kindly by a lord called Munodi. In the country Gulliver saw men working in excellent soil with tools and equipment, but saw no sign of wealth or of an expected harvest. The people lived in poverty and misery. Munodi's estate and the lands surrounding it seemed a haven of greenery and abundance by contrast, for Munodi avoided the new agricultural methods of his neighbors and practised the old-fashioned but proven methods of his fathers.

Munodi informed Gulliver that about 40 years previously, some men had gone up to the floating island on business, acquired a smattering of mathematics and returned to build an academy of projectors in Lagado. All the other towns had since built similar academies, colleges which taught new methods of agriculture and building which promised to enable one man to do the work of ten, to build in one week palaces that would last undeteriorated forever, to increase the crops a hundredfold, and bring numerous other benefits. But, as none of these projects had yet been perfected, the country lay in miserable waste, the houses in ruin, and the people without food or clothes. The projectors, far from discouraged, pursued their interests more madly than ever; but a few gentry, including Munodi, being less enterprising, continued in the old methods and lived in wealth — a circumstance which made them despised by the people. Munodi's house, built by the best ancient rules of architecture, was a noble structure surrounded by gardens, groves, avenues and fountains in perfect taste. As an example of the effects of the new methods, Munodi told Gulliver of an efficient mill formerly on his property that had been turned into a ruin by projectors who had planned to pump water up a mountain to secure the advantage of falling water for turning the mill instead of using the river that already existed. After 100 men had worked two years on the project, it was abandoned, and for seven years since Munodi had received the blame for its failure.

Commentary

The nobleman who assists Gulliver has been thought to represent the Prince of Wales, later George II, in whom the Tories placed hopes of better days. (Compare him with the crown prince in Lilliput.) The Prince of Wales lacked enthusiasm for the musical and scientific interests of his father's court.

Munodi (sometimes identified as Robert Harley, sometimes as Bolingbroke, since each retired to the country and lived in official disgrace after being discharged from high office) is devoted to the good old-fashioned (Tory) ways of doing things, with excellent results, exactly the opposite of the new, untried, ruinous ways of the Whigs. On the agricultural level, this would indicate an endorsement of experience over untried scientific innovations. And, of course, the reader must remember that over all this ruined country hangs the shadow of the withdrawn, distant government of a king and court who rule by science, and lacked all humanity and rapport with the people ruled.

The projectors are not pure scientists, but people who seek to apply science to life without respect for the lessons and wisdom of the past and without sufficient care to discover whether a project, once undertaken, can be successfully completed. Whether Swift intends the projects he discusses to have political or agricultural meaning, the intention is to satirize a headlong dash into novelty and into meddling with established procedures. The old mill has been interpreted as a reference to the history of the South Sea Company. Formed by Harley (a Tory) in 1711, the company agreed to assume £10,000,000 of the national debt in exchange for certain trading rights. All went well until the Whigs renegotiated the contract in a new project by which the company assumed the whole national debt in exchange for greater concessions in 1720. Speculation ran riot. The country suffered one of the most famous market crashes in history, called the South Sea Bubble. Great numbers of people were ruined, and the Whig government was driven from power. Robert Walpole returned to office to salvage the situation.

CHAPTER 5

Summary

Gulliver was well received by the warden of the Academy of Lagado, which contained at least 500 rooms. He saw a man dressed in rags, working on a project to extract sunshine from cucumbers so that man might warm the air on cold summer days. In another room, filled with a repulsive odor, a filthy man was working on a project to reduce human excrement back to its original food. Other researchers were trying to build a house from the roof down, as do the spider and the bee; to produce gunpowder by heating ice; and to plough fields by planting them everywhere with acorns and chestnuts, etc., and letting hogs root them up. This would save the expense of ploughs, draft animals and labor. There were many other experiments proceeding, of equal interest and profit. In another part of the Academy, Gulliver met a projector in speculative learning. Here, he saw a wonderful machine invented by a professor who assured him that anyone could be capable of writing great books on philosophy and the arts with the help of his invention. All that was needed was to operate the machine, which jumbled words into different positions, making new arrangements. Many of these were already collected and bound in volumes. In the school of languages, the professors sought ways of improving their own tongue and writing. They were reducing polysyllables to monosyllables and trying to reduce all language to nouns, omitting the other parts of speech. Their ultimate goal was to abolish all words whatsoever by having man carry around such *things* as they wished to communicate about. Gulliver watched some of these professors as they met in the streets, opened their huge packs of *things*, and use them to converse for an hour at a time. By their method they intended to abolish all language barriers among men. In the mathematics school, students were attempting to learn by eating wafers on which was written the desired knowledge, but as yet the experiment had not succeeded.

Commentary

Marjorie Hope Nicolson in *Science and Imagination* (pages 110-154) deals with Swift's intentions here. He is satirizing the interests and experiments of the Royal Society, some of which are here distorted for Swift's satiric purposes. Even Benjamin Franklin, though a leading scientist of Swift's own century, could satirize the impracticality and wastefulness of researchers proposed by learned societies. (See Franklin's "Letter to the Royal Academy.") The Royal Society was interested in language, in the style of English writing. In his *History of the Royal Society*, Bishop Sprat has a passage that Swift seems to have in mind in his fifth chapter here. The Society has been rigorous, Sprat says, in combating extravagance by exhibiting "a constant Resolution to reject all amplifications, digressions, and swelling of style; to return back to the primitive purity and shortness, when men deliver'd so many *things* almost in an equal number of *words*."

CHAPTER 6

Summary

Gulliver found the school of political projectors distressingly out of their minds, for they proposed that kings should choose their favorites for their wisdom, capacity and virtue; that ministers should promote the public good; that merit, great abilities and eminent services should be rewarded; and, Gulliver said, "many other wild, impossible chimaeras (absurd creations of the imagination) that never entered before into the heart of man to conceive."

One of the professors was more practical. He would treat the diseases that afflict the body politic as physicians treat the natural body. For the first three meeting days of a legislative body he would have physicians study what each senator needed. On the fourth, they would administer the proper medicines. To correct the poor memories of court favorites, he would have their associates jog their memories by giving "a tweak by the nose, or a kick in the belly, or tread on his corns, or lug him thrice by the ears, or run a pin into his breech, or pinch his arm black and blue, to prevent forgetfulness;" and repeat the treatment as often as necessary until the business was accomplished. Senators, he thought, should be obliged to vote contrary to the way they argue, for that way of acting would insure the public good. To end violent party divisions in a state, he would take a hundred leaders from each party, cut their brains in half, and put together for each man two halves of brains from different parties, thus giving the opposing interests a chance for quiet debate and balance within a skull that would bring moderation and quiet to the state.

Two professors argued over how to extract taxes without "grieving" taxpayers. One thought that each man's vices should be taxed, the other that a man should be taxed according to the qualities he esteemed in himself. The highest tax would be on men who were most successful with women, each man's word about his prowess to be taken at face value. Qualities that a man will neither admit in his neighbor nor value in himself (honor, justice, wisdom, learning) should not be taxed at all. Women would be taxed according to (their own opinion of) their beauty and stylish dressing, but constancy, chastity, good sense and good nature would not be considered, since they are too rare to pay for the trouble of finding them.

Another professor exposed the means for discovering plots and conspiracies: examine the diet of suspects, the times of their meals, their sleeping habits, the color of their excrement, which is the key to their thoughts and designs. Gulliver told him of Tribnia (Britain), also called Langden (England), where most of the people are spies, accusers, informers, prosecutors, perjurers, false witnesses and the like, all serving under ministers of state and very skilful in framing whoever it has been decided shall be ruined. They are very clever at deciphering secret meanings in words and in discovering what *other* sentences might be formed out of the letters in one they have.

Commentary

The type of irony has suddenly changed. Here, Swift uses *blame-praise* irony to suggest what he thinks *ought* to be. Formerly, he praised or merely presented things in order to suggest what ought *not* to be. The effect is a sarcastic commentary on the corruptions of government and princes in their discharge of duty. The *right* conduct of public affairs becomes an impossible chimera, something that never entered into man's head. Here, for the first time, Gulliver shows a bitter contempt for the arrangements of his own world. It is this development which makes the passage most noteworthy, and the suddenness of the development, for we have not observed Gulliver in the process of forming the judgment that had to precede such an outburst *against his own nation and kind*.

Gulliver's violence over the political situation surprises us. He seems to have already reversed some of his opinions on his own dear country. By suggesting remedies so radical and shocking he implies that the disease is serious indeed. But the reader must not miss the exuberance of fun that keeps the attack satiric — the amusing list of remedies for the senators ("lenitives, aperitives, abstersives," etc.) or the very extravagance of sawing off and exchanging half-brains between opposite party leaders.

Gulliver — and Swift — have thrown off the air of kindly feeling about humanity. The disapproving sharpness against mankind, the implication that no women are virtuous and no men honorable, sounds a note that will deepen and repeat itself and become a dominant theme as the travels proceed.

In the last section of the chapter, Swift is mocking the methods the Whigs used to discover evidence of treason in the trial of Bishop Atterbury. Twice he suggests the evidence the Whigs had industriously extracted from the bishop's chamber-pot. "The tour" suggests the code name for Bolingbroke, *La Tour*.

CHAPTER 7

Summary

Gulliver decided to sail to the island of Luggnagg as the beginning of a voyage home to England. But, since the Luggnagg ships were not to sail for a month, Gulliver was persuaded to see the wonders on Glubbdubdrib, the Island of Sorcerers and Magicians, where the whole governing tribe were magicians. The governor was served by the dead, whom he had power to command. As he passed through the two rows of guards at the palace, Gulliver's flesh crept with horror. By the turn of his finger, the governor dismissed his servants, who all instantly vanished. A new set of ghosts served at table. Within a day or two Gulliver became perfectly habituated to the presence of spirits. At the governor's invitation Gulliver summoned from the underworld whatever spirits he chose. Alexander the Great declared he had died, not of poison, but of a fever. Hannibal reported that he had not had a drop of vinegar in his camp. The senate of Rome looked like an assembly of demigods, whereas another "assembly of somewhat a latter age" seemed to be a "knot of pedlars, pickpockets, highwaymen and bullies." Gulliver enjoyed the conversation of really noble men, Marcus Brutus, Junius Brutus, Socrates, Epaminondas, Cato the Younger and Thomas More, "a sextumvirate," Gulliver declares, "to which all the ages of the world cannot add a seventh." Gulliver also feasted his eyes on the destroyers of tyrants and usurpers, and the restorers of liberty to nations.

Commentary

Gulliver continues to present comparisons that shrink modern man. Against the Roman senate, that later assembly that must be parliament, of course, seems to be composed of pickpockets and pedlars; and none of the six supreme men of all the ages belongs to Swift's own time. True, Thomas More belonged to England, but to the departed England of the Renaissance. Swift also debunks the stories that pass for history, like those that Hannibal split hot rocks with vinegar and that Alexander the Great was poisoned. Homer, we shall soon hear, was not blind.

CHAPTER 8

Summary

Gulliver had Aristotle and Homer summoned up, at the head of their commentators, but he learned that the two giants had never heard of those followers of theirs, since in the lower world, the commentators, through shame and guilt, always kept as far from the masters as they could. Homer's eyes were "the most quick and piercing" Gulliver had ever beheld. In conversation with Descartes and Gassendi, both modern philosophers, Aristotle proved himself still the king of philosophers by showing how the systems of the two moderns were exploded, and he predicted the same fate for the contemporary favorite theory of attraction.

Summoning up the ghosts of noble families, he was disappointed to find out how short was the history of illustrious lines. Noble families often contained pedlars, barbers, or prelates and could trace their lineage through only a very few generations. Gulliver saw their scandalous secrets laid bare, and he ceased to wonder at the desiccation of the nobility when he saw their blood lines interrupted by "pages, lackeys, varlets, coachmen, gamesters, fiddlers, players, captains and pickpockets."

Modern history disgusted Gulliver most, for he found it totally misrepresented by dishonest writers. Those with heroes' names were cowards; those with wisemen's names were fools; those with reputations for heroic patriotism were traitors. Villains had been exalted to offices of high trust; the virtuous had been executed through the devices of wicked ministers. He discovered the true causes of great events: "how a whore can govern the back-stairs, the back-stairs a council, and the council a senate." He discovered how some had secured high titles and great estates by perjury, fraud, pandering, or prostituting their wives and daughters.

Commentary

Swift's treatment sharply distinguishes between Aristotle and his followers and commentators. There is as great respect for the master as there is contempt for the followers. The theory of attraction for which he has Aristotle predict refutation is Newton's system based on gravitation.

Gulliver fools nobody by his parenthesis "(for I hope the reader need not be told that I do not in the least intend my own country in what

I say upon this occasion)." The remark about prostituting wives and daughters probably reflects on the Duke of Marlborough, that Whig darling, whose rise at court was said to date from the time he delivered his sister up to the future James II. Even Rome, Gulliver learns to his surprise, turned mightily and quickly to corruption once luxury became entrenched there. Needless to say, Swift, through Gulliver, is here raking man's pride again and again, with his special target now the pride of great houses in their ancestry and reputation.

Gulliver amuses the reader who remembers the remarks on the pious Brobdingnagian writer's complaint about the decay of mankind, for now Gulliver's own lament is about how much man has degenerated in the last 300 years. Men today are small, have weaker nerves, and relaxed sinews and muscles. The fine old English yeomen are a race no longer existent, and they are disgraced by the vicious degeneracy of their grandchildren.

CHAPTER 9

Summary

In Luggnagg, Gulliver represented himself as a Dutchman in hopes of getting to Japan, for the Dutch alone of Europeans were received there. To His Majesty of Luggnagg, Gulliver sent the conventional request to have the honor of licking the dust before the royal footstool, but he found the words to be more than mere form. He was commanded to crawl on his belly toward the throne, licking the floor as he went. Gulliver being a stranger, the floor was cleaned for his approach; but those who had powerful enemies at court would find the floor strewn with extra dirt when it was their turn to approach the king. And the king had a brown powder to sprinkle in the paths of those he chose to destroy by a gentle death. The floor-licker in such a case ceased to be troublesome within 24 hours.

Commentary

Swift's favorite travel books, with their stories of Oriental despotism, seem to be mirrored in Gulliver's encounter with this monarch. Swift draws upon fact when he alludes to the unique privileges of the Dutch in Japan. In 1638, after anti-Christian disturbances in Japan, European contacts with the Japanese had to be through Dutch or Chinese traders. By this touch of reality, Swift gives the travels some verisimilitude.

CHAPTER 10

Summary

The Luggnaggians, Gulliver found, were a polite and generous people, though he remarks that they had "some share of that pride which is peculiar to all Eastern countries." With great excitement, Gulliver heard of the *struldbrugs*, immortal men. To any family a child might be born whose forehead was marked with the red circular spot of immortality. "Happy people!" was Gulliver's first reaction, "whose every child may prove to be immortal! Happy nation, blessed with so much ancient wisdom for a guide!" Then he fell into a long dream in which he was a struldbrug. But the Luggnaggians laughed at his ignorance. His glowing plans were all falsely based upon the supposition that the struldbrugs would remain human and not decay beyond the use of either intelligence or body. But, whenever a struldbrug saw a funeral, he enviously wished he might have one, for after passing through an ordinary old age, the struldbrugs continue to decline in every way. They remembered nothing at all, so that at last they could not form a sentence. Thus, they had not even the pleasure of conversation to relieve their evil plight. They were like foreigners in their own country. They were the most mortifying and ghastly sight Gulliver ever beheld, the women being even more horrible than the men.

Commentary

Gulliver strips away another of the vain desires of men. No tyrant, he thinks, could invent a death to which he would not rush, in preference to such a life as struldbrugs live. As he often does, Swift shows that man commonly desires what is bad for himself and neglects his real good. Contemporary medicine in our own time, nevertheless, still frequently speaks about a golden age when life will be prolonged — to two or three hundred years. On the theme of man's pride, Swift reminds man of his mortality and of the truth that since man's physical powers inevitably decay, even mortality is not the worst of evils.

CHAPTER 11

Summary

Before recounting his departure for Japan, Gulliver described the struldbrugs as something out of the ordinary and never yet found in other travel books. He stayed in Japan too short a time to see what the Japanese knew of these unusual creatures, whose existence the extensive trade of Japan with Luggnagg would certainly have revealed to them. Perhaps the Dutch have information on that subject.

The Japanese almost penetrated Gulliver's disguise as a Dutchman because he asked to be excused from the ceremony imposed on the Dutch — that of trampling the crucifix. The emperor suspected Gulliver might be not a real Hollander, but a Christian instead. However, he gave secret orders that his officers should pretend to omit the ceremony through mere forgetfulness, lest Gulliver have his throat cut during the voyage home on a Dutch ship. A meddlesome and malicious Dutchman did, in fact, try to have Gulliver forced to perform the act, and as the Dutch *Amboyna* sailed home, Gulliver had to evade questions about not trampling the crucifix. But he arrived safely in Amsterdam, went thence to the Downs (near Dover), and soon was home after five years and six months away.

Commentary

Gulliver reminds us that we have here a travel book on the same footing as other travellers' reports (only more accurate). He is anxious for the reader to check on the truth of his reports, and he maintains a pretence of verisimilitude by his chain of trading connections from Luggnagg even to England, with whom the Dutch had commerce. But the reader may notice that Swift dared not leave Gulliver in Japan long enough to learn the language and report on life in that nation. It was too much a part of the real world.

Swift's choice of *Amboyna* as the ship's name deliberately continues to fan anti-Dutch sentiments by recalling to English readers the massacre of an English trading settlement at Amboyna in Indonesia, in 1623. The Dutch were probably not required to trample the crucifix, a practice more likely designed to discover Japanese Christians, but Swift does not scruple to distort whatever will serve the purposes of his satire — here, to make the Dutch non-Christians as well as savages.

SUMMARY OF BOOK III

Gulliver's tone in speaking of the world has changed. He now often sounds bitter about the way people and governments act, but he has not turned on man. He is glad to find his wife in good health.

Book III depends upon the relation of wonders more than did the first two books, in which Gulliver was a participant in a continuing story about countries and individuals who were, to a degree, also characters. In Book III, Gulliver moves from place to place seeing things but not getting to know anyone well. Munodi seems about to become a character, but his appearance is brief.

Among the books, this third one has always contained the most mysteries for readers. In his own time Swift was asked to provide a key for it, but he declined. In his famous "Verses on the Death of Dr. Swift, D.S.P.D.," Swift imagines that people will conjecture after his death about the *treason* in his work:

> . . . libels yet conceal'd from sight,
> Against the court to show his spite;
> Perhaps his travels, part the third,
> A lie at every second word —
> Offensive to a loyal ear . . .

The passages in Book III dealing with the revolt of Lindalino were too dangerous for the printer to publish in Swift's time. In fact, they did not become part of the book until 1899, as has been mentioned earlier.

Book IV – A Voyage to the Country of the Houyhnhnms

CHAPTER 1

Summary

After five happy months at home with his wife and children, Gulliver was off again, this time as captain, in his own right, of a 350 ton merchantman. In the West Indies, to replace some of his men who had died, he hired some sailors who proved to be former pirates. They seized the ship. With Gulliver chained and under guard in his cabin, they sailed for some weeks before setting their prisoner ashore with no idea at all of where he was. Soon, he observed some repulsive animals, thickly hairy in some places but with their brown buff skin showing in many others. They had no tails, but had long claws, and climbed trees as nimbly as squirrels. Gulliver instinctively recoiled from them with more aversion than from any other animals he knew of. As he moved along a road, one of these beasts approached him, stared at him, raised one of its forepaws toward him, and for its frightening impertinence received a blow from the flat of Gulliver's sword. Its roar brought forty of the beasts, who howled and made faces around Gulliver, who moved to defend himself with his back to a tree. Some of the creatures, having swung up into the branches above, bombarded Gulliver and almost stifled him with excrement. Suddenly, all the beasts ran away. A horse had approached. He looked with wonder at Gulliver, examined his hands and feet, and blocked Gulliver from leaving the spot, but all very gently. When Gulliver attempted to pet him, the horse shook his head, removed the petting hand with his forefoot, and seemed to neigh something in a language. Another horse came up, greeted the first ceremoniously, and held – so it seemed – a long discussion with the first, obviously about Gulliver.

The two examined Gulliver's hand and clothes with wonder. Their behavior was so orderly and intelligent that Gulliver believed them to be two magicians in the form of horses. He addressed them as magicians, offering a knife and a bracelet to either one for a ride to any house or village. The horses again discussed the situation, frequently using the word *Yahoo* (*yah-hoo* or *yay-hoo*). During a lull in the conversation, Gulliver said "*Yahoo*," to the great surprise of the horses, who taught him the exact pronunciation of that word and of another, *Houyhnhnm* (*whinnum*). Gulliver's learning ability amazed the horses. At last, the horses parted (with ceremony) and Gulliver accompanied the first, a dapple gray.

Commentary

Swift has Gulliver and the reader uncertain about the situation. Gulliver is so revolted at the sight of the first filthy animals that he does not see their resemblance to human beings. And because of the signs of intelligence in the horses, Gulliver expects to find people of extraordinary intelligence governing the country. The horses are quite as mystified by Gulliver as he is by them. Swift keeps us all wondering — Gulliver, horses, and readers alike. We *must* read on.

CHAPTER 2

Summary

After a three-mile walk, Gulliver and the horse entered a low straw-roofed house of timbers stuck upright in the ground and woven across with small branches. The traveller got ready his trinkets as peace offerings to the Indians or whoever should prove to be master of the premises. The horse neighed with authority to three horses and two mares in a smooth clay-floored room and left Gulliver to wait in a second room, where the visitor again prepared his trinkets for the master of the house. He heard the horses conversing in the next room. Gulliver feared his sufferings had disturbed his mind; the adventure seemed impossible. He pinched himself to test whether he was dreaming. But he waited to be taken to the lord of the house. Instead, he was introduced to a lovely mare, a colt, and a foal sitting on well-made straw mats in a third room.

Gulliver was again examined, again heard the word *Yahoo* several times, and then was taken outside to be compared with one of the filthy animals he had first met in this land. To his horror he discovered in that beast "a perfect human figure" with a face flat and broad, the nose depressed, the lips large, the mouth wide, the nails long and strong, and the body hairier than the usual human body. Gulliver's clothes most astonished the horses because they made his body unlike that of the beast. The horses did not recognize that clothes were detachable. With loathing he shrank from the filthy food of the beasts when it was offered to him. He refused hay and oats, and began to fear that he was doomed to starve to death, until he managed to make the gray horse understand that he would drink cow's milk. Fortunately, there was a large store of it in the house, clean, cool, delicious.

An old horse, drawn in a sledge by four Yahoos, arrived for dinner, during which Gulliver was again discussed. Gulliver's gloves perplexed the old horse, at whose wish Gulliver removed them and put them into his pocket. Pleased with his conduct, the horses taught him several new words. With the gray's permission, Gulliver made barley bread to eat. This, with milk, herbs, a little butter and whey from the milk, and an occasional rabbit or bird, kept Gulliver in excellent health during his three years among the horses. He slept in a separate lodge between the house and the Yahoos' stable.

Commentary

Gulliver remarks that there were at this time "few greater lovers of mankind" than he was. But shadows of things to come appear in his linking the remark with a reaffirmation of the horror and disgust the filthy Yahoos inspire in him. He begins to think of man and Yahoo together.

Gulliver justifies discussing his diet by saying that other travel books treat the subject and that his readers might think it impossible for him to subsist in such a country for three years. He is, in reality, pursuing his intention to "flay the world," to strip off the outer coverings of things and expose what lies beneath. In general, what appears to the eye is artificial and wasteful as well as superficial. Here, the suggested artificiality and waste is in food and its preparation, with which men commonly busy, pamper, and sicken themselves by indulgence far beyond what nature demands. The Yahoos' gluttonous and disgusting diet contrasts with Gulliver's simple, healthy fare and suggests the excesses of self-pampering and gluttonous men.

Swift, in Book IV, adds to the literature of a favorite topic among eighteenth-century writers — primitivism, speculation about the nature and worth of human life in pre-civilized times. There are several kinds of primitivism. The type Swift presents shows primitive life as virtuous, simple, reasonable, and therefore healthy, happy and worthy of imitation. A contrasting type of primitivism would be that of the philosopher, Thomas Hobbes, who described early human life as "solitary, poor, nasty, brutish, and short." The Yahoos were not solitary, but the rest of the description fits them: they are not rational, but brute creatures. (On primitivism the student might like to see *A Documentary History of Primitives and Related Ideas* by Arthur O. Lovejoy and others.)

CHAPTER 3

Summary

With diligent effort, Gulliver made swift progress in the Houyhnhnm tongue, assisted by one of the servant horses. Houyhnhnm was, of all languages Gulliver knew, most like high Dutch or German. The master horse continued to be perplexed at Gulliver's un-Yahoolike qualities — his teachableness, civility, cleanliness and clothes. At the end of three months Gulliver could begin to satisfy the Houyhnhnm's curiosity, but the master at first strongly doubted Gulliver's story, sure that he must be saying *the thing that was not* in telling of peoples across the sea, and of wooden vessels controlled by brute Yahoos.

Houyhnhnm (*the perfection of nature*) means "horse." All the Houyhnhnms of the neighborhood came to see the wonderful Yahoo, conversed with him, and helped Gulliver so much that in five months he was master of their tongue. They could not altogether think him a Yahoo, because of his clothes and of some other differences from the beasts. But the secret of Gulliver's clothes was discovered one morning when a servant horse surprised the visitor asleep without them. The master Houyhnhnm could not understand why anyone would be prompted to conceal parts of the body that nature had given. Nevertheless, he allowed Gulliver to remain partly dressed while being examined again. To him, Gulliver appeared a perfect Yahoo despite his smooth, white skin, his shortage of hair, his lack of long claws, and his habit (the Houyhnhnm calls it an "affectation") of walking upright on his "hind" legs. But the main difference was his capacity for speech and reason. Gulliver begged the master not to call him a Yahoo.

As the horse continued to doubt his story, Gulliver at last extracted a promise that the Houyhnhnm would not be offended. Then he informed his host that in all other known countries, men like Gulliver are the presiding rational creatures and horses are brute animals; that Gulliver had been as much surprised to find rational and ruling horses as the Houyhnhnms had been to find a rational Yahoo; and that if Gulliver ever told his own kind about the rational horses and their control of a country, he would be accused of saying *the thing that was not*.

Commentary

The Houyhnhnms, as we shall see, are ruled completely by reason. Therefore, since lying is against the reasonable and natural purpose of speech, the horses have no word for *lying*. Lying is, like rich foods and clothes, a part of the artificial, as contrasted with the natural life. The horses have no need of such a word. Still, reason in them has its limitations. They cannot easily grasp concepts outside their own confined experience: countries other than their own, countries where horses do not rule, ships that are managed by Yahoos.

CHAPTER 4

Summary

The horse was deeply distressed by Gulliver's explanation. Being unused to doubting or not believing, he did not know how to behave when doubts occurred, and he could not comprehend Gulliver's explanation of how men *lie* and *misrepresent*.

When Gulliver described the care, uses and abuses of horses in England, the "master" showed indignation, wondering how Yahoos would dare venture upon a Houyhnhnm's back and expressing a noble resentment on hearing of English horses being beaten, castrated and trained to the service of Yahoos.

The master found Gulliver different from the Yahoos of Houyhnhnm land. Gulliver was cleaner and less "deformed," but had less real advantages than the Yahoos. His nails were of no use; his forefeet were of no use for walking; using only two feet for walking, he was always insecure against falling; his face was flat; the position of his eyes forced him to turn in order to see to the side; he could not feed himself without using a forefoot.

Gulliver's account of his voyage to the country of horses also greatly puzzled the Houyhnhnm, especially the part that explained why pirates dared not return to their native land. Neither could he understand reasons why man committed evils like treason, murder, theft, rape, sodomy, perjury, forgery, poisoning and robbery.

Commentary

The Houyhnhnm's reason rules him. He shows very little passion — a little indignation here and there, but never lust, envy, anger in the violent sense, covetousness, and the other passion-inspired vices by which man too commonly operates. If he has passions, the Houyhnhnm keeps them well disciplined and out of sight. Thus, he cannot comprehend man's lying, a vice which springs from his passions. To the Houyhnhnm, lying is a violation of the natural function of speech. Whatever is natural will be done easily and as a matter of course by the reason-dominated creature.

Gulliver's explanation of these crimes makes the horse ". . . like one whose imagination was struck with something never seen or heard of before . . . lift up his eyes with amazement and indignation." In this passage Swift makes a key point about the whole book of Gulliver: activities that men carry on all the time in measureless superabundance are utterly contrary to reason. To a truly reasonable creature, man's usual conduct would be virtually incomprehensible — and, of course, impossible to carry on.

CHAPTER 5

Summary

At the Houyhnhnm's command, Gulliver related something of English history: the Revolution of 1688; the War of the Spanish Succession, in which perhaps a million died, 100 cities were captured and 500 ships sunk or burned. He discussed the innumerable causes of wars — princely ambition for wider power, corruption of ministers, religious disagreements (the cause of the most furious and bloody wars), anticipation of attack by another country, mutual desire for the same object, a neighbor's weakness resulting from natural disaster or civil strife, opportunity to seize a country after being called in to help defend it, and many others. Some beggarly princes of Europe, too, hired out their citizens to serve other princes for a very large personal profit.

Gulliver continued to educate the horse in man's artificiality. Man does not fight with his natural weapons, nor is he satisfied with merely winning his point. And so the horse learned of firearms and swords, of mines and countermines, of dismemberments and carcasses left to dogs, of plunder and ravishings, and many other details of how men make war. The Houyhnhnm stopped him, afraid that simply by hearing such things he would grow accustomed to them and become corrupted.

The Houyhnhnm master wondered how law, framed to preserve all, could be any man's ruin. Because he thought reason and nature sufficient guides for a rational animal, he was curious about Gulliver's terms *law* and *lawyer*. Gulliver explained that lawyers are men bred to prove, by multiplying words, that black is white and white is black, depending upon how they are paid. As an example, he described litigation over the ownership of a cow, the real owner of which is under serious handicaps because his side is just. Judges are chosen from lawyers who have grown old and lazy and so inveterately used to favoring fraud, perjury and oppression that they have been known to reject bribes from the side where justice lay, in order to avoid doing something unfitting their office or their nature by giving an honest judgment. Since lawyers also enforce a rule that what has been done before may be done again (the principle of *precedent*), they carefully preserve records of every court action against justice and reason so that such actions may be urged as reasons for doing them again, and judges invariably favor the most unjust precedents in their decisions. Lawyers have a jargon of their own, unintelligible to all others. They multiply laws in this jargon, so confounding the essence of truth and falsehood that thirty years are required to decide the simplest cases. Crimes against the state are easily and quickly decided, by having the judge discover whether the rulers desire to have the man hanged or saved, and giving judgment accordingly. Gulliver assured the Houyhnhnm that outside their own specialty, lawyers are far from the brilliant creatures one might suppose and are, in fact, the most ignorant and stupid group in England.

Commentary

Despite being a churchman, Swift is remarkably able to belittle serious religious problems, as he does here and as he did in Book I, where intricate and fundamental religious questions were reduced to which end of an egg should be broken open. Here, dealing with the religious causes of wars, Swift ridicules the controversy over Christ's real presence in the consecrated species as a question of whether bread be flesh or wine be blood. The Cross becomes a post.

But the overall discussion concerns wars and their causes, in which the Houyhnhnm finds what he ironically calls the effects of the reason Gulliver pretends to. But, still unaware of the artificial means by which wars are carried on, he finds comfort in thinking that the Yahoos Gulliver represents, considering their poor natural equipment, can do no very great damage to one another, and therefore Gulliver's account of the losses in war must the *the thing which is not*.

Before becoming king of England, George I had rented mercenary troops to other princes. Swift treads near trouble in his remarks about the practice.

The Houyhnhnm finds man worse and more detestable than the Yahoos. He sees in man, not reason, but the corruption of reason. That corruption, he fears, is worse than brutality itself. Gulliver will repeat the theme: man abuses reason by making it the servant, not the master, of his passions.

Gone is the Gulliver eager to make his country appear better than the facts warrant. Gone also is the Gulliver who can look upon England with an indulgent eye. His every descriptive stroke now is a lash — for lawyers, foreign policy, court system, or anything else English. He has lived with the strictly honest and rational Houyhnhnm for so long now that the abuses of reason and nature have become easily apparent to him. The reasonable and natural purpose of law and courts is to insure justice, and against this simple principle Gulliver judges what actually happens in courts.

CHAPTER 6

Summary

Gulliver explained the use of money, and how its possession permitted an English Yahoo to obtain whatever he wanted — the choicest clothing, land, food and females. This power of money moved Yahoos to accumulate as much of it as possible. But, as money was power, a thousand poor labored to live miserably in order to support one rich man in plenty. This arrangement the Houyhnhnm could not comprehend, supposing that all animals had a right to their share of earth's products. Gulliver's description of trade — "that this whole globe of earth must be at least three times gone round, before one of our better female Yahoos could get her breakfast or a cup to put it in" — also caused the horse to wonder. How could so large a land be without fresh water, so that the inhabitants must send overseas for drink? Gulliver explained how England sends her large surplus of food and drink overseas to trade for the materials of diseases, folly, and vice, to supply the intemperance of her males and the vanity of her females. *Wine*, he explained, was not to *replace* water, but to "make us merry by putting us out of our senses," suspend the operation of reason for a time, and deprive the drinker of the use of his limbs.

Diseases and physicians were hard for the Houyhnhnm to comprehend, for it seemed impossible that nature should allow pains to develop in natural bodies. Gulliver explained the physical evils that follow unwise eating and drinking, and those that accompany consorting with diseased prostitutes. Being a physician, Gulliver unveiled the whole mystery of curing the sick. Since basically all diseases spring from repletion (over-fullness), the first remedy is evacuation — either downwards or upwards; the next is to induce a vomit by fashioning from the most repulsive ingredients the most nauseous mixture imaginable, or by an equally disgusting remedy to secure a purge downwards. For imaginary diseases (the favorite type in females), physicians apply imaginary cures. They are very skilled at prognosticating death, which they can always bring about although they cannot always keep it away. They are very useful to those who wish to be rid of their mates, to eldest sons, to government ministers and to princes.

A first or chief minister of state Gulliver presented as:

> ... a creature wholly exempt from joy and grief, love and hatred, pity and anger; at least made use of no other passions but a violent desire of wealth, power, and titles; ... he applies his words to all uses, except to the indication of his mind; ... he never tells a *truth* but with an intent that you should take it for a *lie*; nor a lie but with a design that you should take it for a *truth*; ... those he speaks worst of behind their backs are in the surest way of preferment; and whenever he begins to praise you to others or to yourself, you are from that day forlorn. The worst mark you can receive is a *promise*, especially when it is confirmed with an oath; after which every wise man retires, and gives over all hopes.

To secure the office of chief minister a man may: 1) profitably dispose of a wife, a daughter, or a sister; 2) betray or undermine his predecessor; or 3) show a furious zeal against court corruption. The third approach betrays the one for the prince to choose, for those who use it always prove to be the most subservient to the monarch's desires. The chief minister's power is perpetuated by wholesale bribery, and punishment for misdeeds in office is eliminated by what is called an Act of Indemnity. The house of a chief minister is a breeding ground for future chief ministers: pages, lackeys, porters, all learn by imitation to excel in insolence, lying, bribery, the most necessary ingredients. First ministers are usually ruled by some "decayed wench or footman," the true ruler of the country and the channel of all favors.

Finding Gulliver superior to the Yahoos in shape, color and cleanliness, and also in having speech and the beginnings of reason, the Houyhnhnm supposed his guest to be of noble family in his own country. Gulliver corrected the horse's notions of nobility, which in England, he said, meant being bred in idleness and luxury, consuming one's vigor and contracting diseases among odious females and, after ruining one's fortune, marrying a meanly born, disagreeable, physically unsound female merely for her money. The children of such unions were generally sickly and deformed, unless the wife had found them a healthy father among her servants or neighbors. Noble blood is so commonly known by a sickly appearance that a healthy nobleman is suspected to have been fathered by a coachman or a groom. The minds of the nobility match their feeble bodies. But the assembly of nobles is the court of highest appeal in England, and no law can be enacted without its consent.

Commentary

Having firmly established the principles of reason and nature as background to what he reports of England, Swift simply describes the "facts." The satire will take care of itself, for the reader is always comparing what *is* with what nature and reason indicate *ought to be*.

Walpole is, of course, the target of this furious description, for, in England, *first minister* meant Walpole. But the satire would fail to be universal if it spent its energy on one poor Walpole. Instead, the passage is phrased to suggest all first ministers and master politicians, and echoes an attitude towards politicians that is as old as politics and was a favorite topic with writers of Swift's day, especially Tory writers.

CHAPTER 7

Summary

Gulliver explained why he could deliver an honest account of his own species among the Houyhnhnms, who were naturally disposed to think the worst of mankind. The virtues of the horses, contrasted with the corruptions of mankind, had opened his eyes and understanding. He now saw man's actions and passions in a new light and found man's honor unworthy and incapable of defence before the sharply intelligent Houyhnhnm.

Further, Gulliver decided never to return to his kind but to live and die surrounded by the virtuous example of the noble horses. Yet — to our surprise — he declared that as things turned out, he was glad that he did give as favorable an account of man as the facts would allow.

The master Houyhnhnm concluded, after meditating over Gulliver's story, that Gulliver's people were animals who, having received a small pittance of reason, used it only to increase their natural corruptions. They had cast away their natural advantages and multiplied unnecessary wants, which they spent their lives vainly trying to supply. Even Gulliver, he now decided, was inferior to the Yahoo in natural strength, speed, agility and other qualities. Law and government among men he attributed to defects in reason, since true reason was sufficient to govern men, and he believed that Gulliver's account had often concealed the truth. He found men also like the Yahoos in their disposition of mind, for the Yahoos hated each other more than they did any other species. The reason usually given for this had been the odiousness of their shapes, and the master had therefore thought it "not unwise for men to cover their bodies." But now, he thought the Yahoos, like Gulliver's kind, detested each other because each one wanted to *have all to itself*. He described how the Yahoos would fight over a cow's carcass though, lacking the weapons of Europeans, they seldom killed one another. They coveted and hid away shining stones, and were out of sorts and downright ill when the stones were missing. The fiercest Yahoo battles occurred in fields abounding in those stones. He found a likeness to English lawsuits in the observed fact that while two Yahoos were fighting over the ownership of a stone, a third would carry it off for himself.

The Houyhnhnm thought nothing in the Yahoos more odious than their undistinguishing gluttony, their preference for eating what they stole at some distance, or their habit of sucking a certain root that affected them as wine did the European Yahoos. The Yahoos, Gulliver observed, were the only animals in the country subject to any diseases, owing to the nastiness and greediness of the sordid brutes. The cure for the *Yahoo's evil* is a mixture of dung and urine, forced down the patient's throat. Gulliver recommended it as a tested remedy for diseases produced by overeating.

For learning, government, arts and manufactures, the Houyhnhnm found no parallel among the Yahoos unless it was the possession by the ruling Yahoo in each band of a favorite (always the most deformed and mischievous) whose office was *to lick his master's feet and posteriors and drive the females to his kennel*. The favorite, hated by the whole herd, held office till a worse could be found, and when he lost favor, was covered entirely by the excrement of all the district's Yahoos.

In fairness, however, the Houyhnhnm pointed out that some Yahoo traits were not evidently paralleled in Gulliver's own people. The Yahoos held their females in common like other animals; the pregnant females admitted the males, as other animals do not; and they loved nastiness and dirt, unlike any other animal. Gulliver said nothing to these observations, because on the first two he could not claim a distinction for man, and on the third there were no hogs in the country to rival the filthiness of Yahoos. The master could not explain the conduct of young Yahoos who, seemingly healthy and needing nothing, hid away and howled until they were brought to their senses by being put to hard work.

The Houyhnhnm also described some habits of the female Yahoos in which Gulliver discerned "with some amazement, and much sorrow, that the rudiments of lewdness, coquetry, censure and scandal, should have place by instinct in womankind." The Yahoos, however — and Gulliver again keeps the information from his master — are too near nature to have developed the unnatural vices of man.

Commentary

Truth is the bug that has bitten Gulliver, who declares he has learned "an utter detestation of all falsehood or disguise, and Truth appeared so amiable to me that I determined upon sacrificing everything to it."

Gulliver does not inform the Houyhnhnm, but he observes to himself that a court of equity would not let the litigants escape so easily. The court would continue the case until neither contestant had anything left. The English facts are thus again worse than reason would conceive them to be. Gulliver's silence on the subject justifies his previous statement that he gave the Houyhnhnm as favorable an account as the facts permitted.

CHAPTER 8

Summary

Having a great desire to observe the Yahoos for himself, Gulliver received permission to walk among them, accompanied by one of the master's servants, a strong sorrel nag. He found them to be nimble creatures who constantly gave off a disgusting odor. Because they were cunning, cruel, stupid and cowardly, they never became more than animals of burden. The red-haired ones were more mischievous than the rest. Gulliver was mortified one day when a young female, inflamed with desire, leapt into a stream where Gulliver was bathing, embraced him violently, and let go her hold only with the greatest reluctance when a servant horse came to the rescue. The horses were greatly amused by the incident.

Among the Houyhnhnms, the principal effort was to cultivate reason. By reason they so lived and acted that they had no idea of what evil in a rational creature could be. And since, with them, truth was instantly and clearly obvious, they had no conception of the meaning of *opinion*, nor could they argue the plausibility of both sides of a case. The master horse laughed at Gulliver's presenting several systems of natural philosophy, because to the horse it seemed ridiculous that one pretending to reason should concern himself with other people's conjectures. The horses cultivated friendship and benevolence as principal virtues, extending them to friend and stranger alike. They practised decency and civility, but had no ceremony. They had no *special* love for their colts, but by the direction of reason they valued most those who were eminent in virtue. They produced two colts to a family and then ceased to practise marital relations. Servant-class families were allowed to produce three children of each sex, to insure a sufficient number of domestics for noble families. Their marriages were arranged very reasonably, with a care to choose colors that would mix well. They had no ideas — nor words for them — of love, courtship, presents, or marriage settlements, but marriage they regarded as a necessity imposed by reason and undertaken because family and friends approved of it. Among them marriage was never violated, though each partner bore the same friendship and benevolence towards the other as he did towards all Houyhnhnms.

Young Houyhnhnms were all reared to temperance, industry, exercise, strength, speed, and hardiness, females as well as males. (Gulliver's master thought it monstrous that English females should — except for small domestic skills — receive an education different from that of males.) Four times a year in each district, a prize was awarded, a song in the victor's honor, to the young Houyhnhnm who showed the greatest skills in physical exercises.

Every fourth year a representative council of the nation met to consider the problems of the country and remedy all of them.

Commentary

Gulliver suffers horrible mortification. He fears now that he is a real Yahoo, since the female shows a natural inclination for him. But Gulliver does not realize that, conversely, he feels *anything but* an inclination for her. Thus, Swift seems to stand apart from Gulliver, allowing *him* to confound himself with the filthy brutes, while Swift reserves his own judgment and permits us to make our own.

The Houyhnhnm life, though appropriate to animals lacking man's passions, can hardly be intended as a literal suggestion of how man shall live. But, in the Houyhnhnms, Swift has isolated for serious consideration the rational part that supposedly distinguishes man from the brutes. Swift seems to be saying, "If man were rational, if he could truly be ruled by reason, he would live as do the noble horses;" and, thus considered, the Houyhnhnm life *is* relevant in man's self-examination, self-judgment and determination toward reform. Man *could* live somewhat nearer the ideal of pure reason.

CHAPTER 9

Summary

Near the end of Gulliver's stay in Houyhnhnm land, a great council of the horses gathered to debate the only real question they ever considered: whether to exterminate the Yahoos. Borrowing from Gulliver's account of how horses are managed in England, the master Houyhnhnm proposed that the young of the Yahoos be castrated so that they would be rendered tame and that in a generation the race of Yahoos would cease to exist. Meanwhile, he urged, the Houyhnhnms should cultivate asses, more tractable and comelier beasts, to perform the small services required. Other things were discussed which concerned Gulliver, but of these he was not informed at the time.

Having no written language, the Houyhnhnms kept all their knowledge by tradition. They had little history to remember, because nothing happened. They had no international or commercial relations, and their people were reasonable and orderly. They had no diseases and no physicians, but they had effective herbs for dressing accidental cuts and bruises. They measured the year by sun and moon, knew of eclipses, but had very little knowledge of astronomy. In poetry they excelled all other mortals, Gulliver judged. Their buildings, rude and simple, were yet well contrived for the climate, being woven of oat straw or wattles around pointed upright stakes in the ground. With their forefeet they were remarkably skilful at even such small tasks as threading needles.

Barring accidents, the Houyhnhnms died only of old age, and they died very reasonably, without either joy or grief on their own part or that of their relatives. They lived to 70 or 75, but rarely to 80 years, knowing by the onset of a general decay that they would survive but a few weeks. Then they received visits from their friends, and near the end they went about themselves to take a last farewell before quietly falling asleep. The only term they had to denote a deficiency was the word *Yahoo*, which they added to the name of the defective thing. Thus, *Yoholmhn-rohlnw Yahoo* meant an "ill-contrived house."

CHAPTER 10

Summary

Gulliver had nicely settled into living in Houyhnhnm land. All his problems of food, clothing, furniture and housing were solved, and he had convinced himself that *nature is very easily satisfied* and that *necessity is the mother of invention*. His health was perfect, his mind at ease, his life free from the annoyances and humiliations of a corrupted society. He had the advantage of listening to the noble horses. He spoke only when asked to and did it with regret, because during his own speech he could not listen to the noble Houyhnhnms. He found that the master understood Yahoos better than Gulliver himself did. "He went through all our vices and follies," reports the narrator.

Suddenly, when Gulliver had settled for living out a happy life among the horses, he received an agonizing message: the Houyhnhnm assembly had decreed that he must leave. The representatives had taken offense at the gray horse's keeping a Yahoo as if he were a Houyhnhnm. They were afraid to force him to live with the Yahoos because with his rudimentary reasoning ability, he might organize the depraved beasts into systematized raiding of the Houyhnhnm's cattle. Gulliver's master was distressed at losing Gulliver, but the neighbors' pressure was too much to withstand.

Gulliver expected to perish trying to leave the country, and he shrank from any return to his own odious kind, yet he agreed to leave. In six weeks' time, with the help of a servant horse, Gulliver constructed a canoe covered with Yahoo skins and a sail of the same material. He stocked his boat with boiled rabbit flesh and other provisions, kissed the master's foot and sailed towards an island he could see about five leagues away.

Commentary

Here, Gulliver clearly shows that he has in his own mind become a Yahoo and identifies all men as Yahoos. He has acquired the feeling of respect and awe which all other animals display towards the horses, and he is grateful that creatures so exalted will deign to accept him among them. He thinks of Europeans as Yahoos in shape and disposition, a little more civilized and possessing speech, perhaps. But the Houyhnhnm has discovered that the principal use of what man calls "reason" is put to no other use among men than to "improve and multiply" what vices nature had given. Gulliver has so grown to hate the Yahoos' form that he turns away in loathing from his own reflection in a pool. He has learned to trot like a horse, and still takes it as a great compliment when friends notice the trait.

The unfeeling decision of the horses measures how far pure reason can go in successfully managing human life. Had Gulliver the passionless nature of the horses, he could and would accept the assembly's decision without disturbance. Instead, he faints. Yet Gulliver had lived long enough among the Houyhnhnms to agree with the wisdom and justice of their action as they see it. The assembly's resolution was not a command but an exhortation to the Houyhnhnm master to banish Gulliver, for the horses cannot understand how a rational creature can be compelled to act. He can be exhorted or advised. And the master feels the pressure of the exhortation.

Gulliver is grateful for the marked favor the Houyhnhnm extends to him at parting by raising his hoof so that Gulliver need not reach to the ground to kiss it. Gulliver has achieved a kind of humility, but another view of his parting convicts Gulliver of an unbalanced mind. Parting from a horse, he kisses its foot.

CHAPTER 11

Summary

After a tender parting from his Houyhnhnm friends, Gulliver considered his plans. He hoped to find an uninhabited island on which he could support himself for life. Returning to civilization, with its corruptions and its incitements to renewed viciousness, seemed an intolerable notion to him. On the island to which he made his way, he was pursued by savages and wounded in the knee by an arrow. He saw a sail but fled from it as threatening his return among men, and he paddled into the neighborhood of the savages again. But the ship sent a party of men ashore to get water. Four of them found Gulliver hiding, spoke to him in Portuguese, wondered at his odd clothes and at his explanations about Yahoos and Houyhnhnms, and laughed over his horselike neighing tone. Meanwhile, Gulliver trembled in fear and hatred.

The Portuguese captain, Pedro de Mendez, Gulliver described as "a very courteous and generous person," yet Gulliver answered his civilities with sullen silence. And the smell of the captain nearly caused him to faint. He tried to leap overboard, but was prevented and was chained in his cabin. Captain Mendez showed such civil and moving concern about Gulliver that, at last, his difficult guest condescended to treat him as a creature having some little portion of reason.

Bound by an oath not to attempt to destroy himself, Gulliver spent most of the voyage to Lisbon shut up in his cabin away from the crew. He shunned wearing clothes touched by Yahoos. He would not wear even a new suit until he had aired it for twenty-four hours. In Lisbon, he had himself led backwards up to the highest room in Captain Mendez' house. The captain patiently tried to persuade Gulliver to accept his own kind again, so far succeeding that at last Gulliver was induced to walk in the street — with his nose stopped up with rue or tobacco to keep out the Yahoo smells. He yielded to the captain's urgings that as a matter of honor and conscience he should return home. The sight of his family revolted him. He fainted at his wife's embrace. For a year he could not bear the presence of his family. "To this hour," he said, "they dare not presume to touch my bread," nor would he permit them to take him by the hand. For five years he lived in the stable, talked with the horses, and of all men welcomed only the groom — because he smelled like a horse.

Commentary

Even though Swift has prepared well for this encounter, the reader is perhaps surprised by Gulliver's reactions of hatred, fear and revulsion at meeting men of his own kind. Among the horses, we remember, he shrank in loathing from his own reflection in water. Three years with the Houyhnhnms have now so accustomed Gulliver to think of his own kind as animals that the conversation of the Portuguese seems as unnatural to him as that of dogs would be.

Gulliver exhibits a curiously split approach to his experience here. He describes the kindly treatment he receives from the Portuguese sailors. He describes Captain Mendez as a paragon of charity and good breeding. Yet Gulliver, pretending to nearly infinite superiority because of his contact with the Houyhnhnms, shows himself a boor by contrast with Mendez, and is surly, sullen, full of hate. By comparison, Captain Mendez is far the more rational of the two, far the closer of the two to the Houyhnhnm ideal. Gulliver's mind is seriously unhinged. He suffers from what the Greeks called *hybris*, an arrogant pride characterized by a man's stepping out of his proper place in the world. Gulliver's place is that of a man. He acts as though he were a Houyhnhnm — or a god — immeasurably above his own kind. Traditionally, *hybris* has been quickly followed by death or other serious punishment. The developing paradox of Gulliver is that in his pride, his theme will be a violent denunciation of man's pride — all men's pride except his own.

Gulliver continues to give evidences of his madness and his pride. He arrogantly tells Captain Mendez that in return for the latter's favors he will "give so much allowance to the corruptions of his nature" as to answer the Captain's difficulties over the strange story Gulliver has told. He reports that his terror of men gradually lessened, but his hatred and contempt increased. He states that on meeting his family, his feelings towards them were "hatred, disgust, and contempt;" and at the idea of having copulated with a Yahoo to produce more of them, his reactions are "shame, confusion, and horror." But his memory and imagination are "perpetually filled with the virtues and ideas of those exalted Houyhnhnms." His pursuit of reason and virtue have made him a raving monomaniac, and so he lives with the horses.

CHAPTER 12

Summary

In the farewell to the reader, Gulliver first insisted on his total truthfulness. He gave only plain fact because he intended to inform, not amuse. A traveller's chief business, he announced, should be to make men wiser, not dazzle them with wonders. And Gulliver wished for a law requiring an oath of travellers that what they publish is true. After the Houyhnhnm experience, Gulliver could not be made to swerve one degree from strict truth. He did expect that future travellers might detect errors of fact in his descriptions of the countries he had found and so "jostle him out of vogue" and make the world forget him. Such eclipse would be a great mortification if he wrote for fame, but his sole intention has been the public good. That intention was proven by his mere presentation of the virtues of the noble Houyhnhnms, which will necessarily shame men in their vices.

Gulliver justified his not registering the countries he discovered for the Crown of Great Britain by saying that Lilliput is not worth subjugating and that the other lands would be too dangerous to attack. He rather wished that the Houyhnhnms might send out missionaries to civilize Europe by teaching it their virtues. Besides, he has had visions of the brutality and injustice by which new dominions are acquired (with a title of *divine right*) and *modern colonies* set up. England, of course, was innocent of all such barbarity. He had so far reapproached humankind as to allow his wife to sit with him at the far end of a long table and answer (briefly!) a few questions. He still, however, had to stuff his nose against the Yahoo smell. And he put into one strong statement what he singled out as the principal fault in man:

> I am not in the least provoked at the sight of a lawyer, a pickpocket, a colonel, a fool, a lord, a gamester, a politician, a whoremonger, a physician, an evidence, a suborner, an attorney, a traitor, or the like: this is all according to the due

course of things: but when I behold a lump of deformity and diseases, both in body and mind, smitten with *pride*, it immediately breaks all the measures of my patience; neither shall I be ever able to comprehend how such an animal and such a vice could tally together.

In his own humility he pleaded with those who had "any tincture of this absurd vice" not to "presume to appear" in his sight.

Commentary

But a very significant sentence here interrupts the course of Gulliver's thoughts. "I shall say nothing of those remote nations where Yahoos preside; amongst which the least corrupted are the Brobdingnagians, whose wise maxims in morality and government it would be our happiness to observe." Here, it seems, is the real message of *Gulliver's Travels*, as Swift sends us back to reconsider a different but noble model for our conduct and institutions. The Brobdingnagians are real men, with passions like ours. And, unlike the horses, they are models for imitation. Their morality and government are "wise," and so man is urged once again to be "big," to think and act like a giant, not like a Lilliputian nor like a Yahoo — nor should he madly try to think himself a Houyhnhnm.

Gulliver's delusions continue as he praises himself as an author, totally free from every error charged to common writers. He claims to write without passion, prejudice, or ill will, solely for the information and instruction of mankind, over which he "without a breach of modesty" claims superiority because of having conversed with the Houyhnhnms.

SUMMARY OF BOOK IV

Book IV contains Swift's most savage castigation of man's perverted ways. Judged by the standard of passion-free reasonableness, man's conduct from beginning to end is monstrous. Man thinks himself reasonable, a *rational animal*. Gulliver claims instead that the rational and animal qualities are completely disparate. He finds reason in a practical sense isolated as a standard, as an ideal, and as an operating principle in the horses, who are so little animal that they seem to be reason incarnate. In the Yahoos he finds animality uncontrolled by reason, and of the two alleged parts of man's nature he finds the brute part the recognizably human one. Living by reason appears to be impossible to man, and the reader discovers, as a sort of clinching proof of the fact, that Gulliver, the man most passionately desirous of living by reason, in the very effort loses his reason and goes mad.

But though man cannot live by pure reason, since he *is* a creature of passions, a less difficult and more easily imitated model is offered to him: the noble Brobdingnagians, whose moral stature calls man to rise above his Lilliputian pettiness and Yahoo filthiness by fixing his mind and his desires on large ideas and large ends. Thus, the book offers a positive program for man.

Gulliver's Postscript: A Letter from Capt. Gulliver to his Cousin Sympson

Nine years after *Gulliver's Travels* first appeared, Swift included in the 1735 Dublin edition a letter from Gulliver to his cousin Sympson, the "publisher" of the book. Whether this letter appears as it did in the 1735 *Travels*, printed at the front of the book, or whether it is placed at the end, as it frequently is now, the letter should be considered Gulliver's postscript, his last reflections and his last word on the *Travels*. It is dated 1727.

Summary

Gulliver reproaches his cousin for publishing a version of the *Travels* that is not only "very loose and uncorrect" (so much Gulliver had agreed to allow), but is, in addition, guilty of omitting things and — worse — adding material that was not his. These additions Gulliver renounces, particularly a paragraph dealing with the reign of Queen Anne. He charges serious omissions and the mangling of several passages of his discourse with the Houyhnhnms. On the whole, he declares, he scarcely recognizes the book as his own. He notes and contradicts a former excuse of Sympson's, that the authorities were quick to pounce upon the smallest innuendoes from the press. Gulliver also complains of his own lack of judgment in publishing the voyages. He recalls having resisted Sympson's call to serve the *public good* by maintaining that the Yahoos were animals utterly incapable of change for the better. And how right he had been appears from the results:

> . . . instead of seeing a full stop put to all abuses and corruptions in this little island, as I had reason to expect: behold, after above six months warning, I cannot learn that my book hath produced one single effect according to my intentions: I desired you would let me know by a letter, when party and faction were extinguished; judges learned and upright; pleaders honest and modest, with some tincture of common sense; and Smithfield blazing with pyramids of law-books; the young nobility's education entirely changed; the physicians banished; the female Yahoos abounding in virtue, honour, truth and good sense; courts and levees of great ministers thoroughly weeded and swept; wit, merit, and learning rewarded; all disgracers of the press in prose

and verse condemned to eat nothing but their own cotton, and quench their thirst with their own ink. These and a thousand other reformations, I firmly counted upon by your encouragement; as indeed they were plainly deducible from the precepts delivered in my book. And, it must be owned, that seven months were a sufficient time to correct every vice and folly to which Yahoos are subject, if their natures had been capable of the least disposition to virtue or wisdom. . . .

So far from reformation is the country that, on the contrary, Yahoos are loading the mails every week with libels against Gulliver, keys to the *Travels*, reflections and memoirs on the *Travels*, and even additions to them, attacks on Gulliver for "reflecting" on persons in power, for denigrating human nature and abusing the female sex. Some attribute the *Travels* to other writers.

The printer has changed the dates, even the years, of events in the *Travels*, and since the original copy is reported destroyed, Gulliver offers corrections for any new edition to be published. If some sea-Yahoos find fault, as he hears some do, with his sea-language, Gulliver can do nothing about it but use the language he learned from old mariners in his youth. Language fashions change on the sea as well as elsewhere, so that now Gulliver cannot understand the sea-Yahoos who visit him.

If Yahoo opinions could affect Gulliver, he might complain of those who think his *Travels* a fiction, especially the accounts of Houyhnhnms and Yahoos. None challenge the existence of Lilliput and Brobdingnag. Why should they hold him less truthful about the other, especially when Yahoos swarm on every street every day? Do they, moreover, expect him to defend his truthfulness? All Houyhnhnmland knows that in two years there, he totally eradicated his tendencies to lying and deceits.

But he will no longer trouble himself or anybody else with a project he would never have undertaken unless some of his Yahoo corruptions had begun to return, the project of reforming Yahoos, an absurd and visionary scheme.

Commentary

This is Swift's humorous postscript, but not only that. He earlier and elsewhere complained that his book had been changed by publishers, as indeed it had. From its first printing even the authorized editions suffered as Gulliver here complains they did. But the instant popularity of the book spawned psuedo-Gullivers, keys to Gulliver, and a spurious text that contained a voyage of return to Brobdingnag. As was noted previously, Swift had reason to fear for his printer's ears. He could hardly have been surprised to find that the printer himself valued them too — enough to beware of passages an unfriendly government might construe as treason. It was still (1726) less than two years since Swift had led the defeat of the government's effort to impose Wood's coinage on Ireland. Walpole's Whigs might well be glad of a chance to punish the troublemaker, especially when they themselves were a favorite target of the satiric thrusts in the *Travels*.

Character Sketches

Introduction

Simply put, a character is a "person" in a story. Characterization is the author's depiction of the character by a choice of images that presents the person, his actions, his ways of thinking and living, and above all, his qualities of mind, heart and will. Nothing in a narrative, generally speaking, matches character in importance, for the traits of the people concerned generate the action and dialogue, carry the conflict, engage the sympathies or aversions of readers, and in their march to a denouement produce the suspense that holds readers to the story.

Students should be alert to notice *how* the writer presents his characters:

- Does the writer merely *tell* the qualities and appearance of the character? This is hardly a subtle way, and unless the writer is extremely skilful, his work will lack interest.
- Does he let the reader infer from the character's *actions* what the qualities of the "person" must be?
- Does he do it by tuning in on the character's speech, his verbal contacts with others?
- Does he let the reader into the mind of the character, so that the thoughts there will reveal the man?
- Does he mix some or all of these methods? Most writers do.

Note also whether characters are *static* (unchanging) or *dynamic* (developing). Dynamic characters may change for better or for worse. In *Gulliver's Travels*, the main character is dynamic, as may easily be seen by comparing the good-natured, patriotic Gulliver of Book I with the horse-mad, hater of Yahoos at the end of Book IV. The supporting characters are static. The Lilliputian emperor, the Brobdingnagian king, Glumdalclitch, Gulliver's Houyhnhnm master all remain unchanged as the story progresses, as also does Captain Mendez. If the Lilliputian emperor seems to grow different, it is not that *he* changes or develops but that the reader's understanding of him becomes clearer. At first, he seems admirable, but like the kingdom over which he rules, an inner corruption is manifest on better acquaintance.

Few characters in *Gulliver's Travels* function importantly in the action. Aside from any need merely to identify them, such persons as Clefren Frelock and Marsi Frelock, who search Gulliver in Lilliput and report their findings, may safely be ignored as of little or no consequence to developments in the book. The same is true of many other people who are but names that come momentarily before the reader: Gulliver's ship captains, the Governor of Luggnagg, Gulliver's wife Mary, or James Bates, his master-surgeon instructor in London.

Gulliver

In Book I, Gulliver unfolds his history and education. He is an ordinary, good man, not rich, the son of a small country landholder. He must scrape and save in order to be educated as a surgeon. He follows the sea. In Lilliput, he shows himself good-natured and gentle with the tiny people. He assists in their war against Blefuscu, not injuring any "enemies," but depriving them of instruments for inflicting damage and injury. Immediately, he shows a noble generosity and respect for the liberty of others by refusing to enslave the Blefuscudians. The treacherous intrigue against him, ensuing from this refusal, gives Gulliver a choice of destroying the Lilliputians, submitting to their barbarous intentions, or fleeing. To his credit he does not seriously consider destroying his miniscule enemies. He flees. Gulliver has won the confidence of the reader as being trustworthy, a man of integrity, uprightness, sound judgment, and humanity. He is a solid Englishman. The reader is perfectly satisfied with the health of his intellect and judgment. There has been no occasion to raise any questions of that nature, and Gulliver has reacted well to the situations he has met. It was important that Swift have so sound a man as his hero. The changes he will undergo because of his experiences have more meaning in this way than they would if they occurred to a man of less solid mind and judgment.

Gulliver's experiences in Brobdingnag begin to change his character. Subject to constant humiliations in the land of the giants, he develops defences for his self-esteem. He boasts what he *would have done* to the monkey *if* he had thought of using his sword; he glories in the seamanship he exhibits to the court ladies; he attempts to show his physical prowess in the unfortunate affair of the cowdung. But it is the sharp-witted, keen-eyed Brobdingnagian king who most puts him on the defensive, and the effects on Gulliver are worth noticing. Gulliver confides to the reader that through partiality to his native land he has suppressed many a truth that would make England appear inferior in the eyes of his giant listener. To put it another way, he has begun to shuffle and lie. He seems less trustworthy than he formerly did. And now, also, Gulliver develops a defensive stubborn vanity, a contempt for things Brobdingnagian, that undermines his ability to perceive values and undercuts our respect for him. He is much less generous in viewing others than we had taken him to be; he is grudging in admitting the goodness of what is non-English; we may suspect he will treat us as he does the giant king by not reporting all that might show Brobdingnag to advantage. Details of this development are seen in his patronizing sneer at the king's view as "the miserable effects of a confined education;" in his contempt for the king's integrity in rejecting gunpowder and tyranny over his country; in his disdain of the king's rejecting "mystery, refine-ment, and intrigue" in government; in his scorn of Brobdingnagian education.

The change in Gulliver has destroyed our trust in his judgment and his strict honesty. We must henceforth weigh his pronouncements carefully.

During Book III, Gulliver's character remains static. He observes and reports what he sees, but his character is not affected. His deepest experience in that book brings a change of opinion and desire, not one of character. He will never again desire to prolong his old age.

But Book IV resumes where Book II left off. Gulliver is a changing, dynamic character. In the second chapter comes his shattering recog-nition that the Yahoo has the "perfect human figure." By the fifth chapter, Gulliver's struggle to escape seeing himself as a Yahoo and his association with the Houyhnhnms have produced a man no longer inclined to represent his country as better than it is. He may not volunteer some details that would worsen the horse's ideas of England, but his accounts of lawyers, courts, nobles, physicians, politicians, and what-not will no longer be praising or excusing. Rather than soften the picture, even of his own profession, he will describe physicians as very useful to husbands and wives who wish to get rid of their mates, or to eldest sons who wish to inherit property. He falls in love with the life of the Houyhnhnms. No blow could be harsher to him than the order to leave the land of the horses. Rather than return to men, he prefers to risk drowning.

As Gulliver returns among men, it clearly emerges that he is seriously unhinged and a thoroughly changed character. Instead of the good-natured Gulliver, there is one whose ill-nature can scarcely be matched. Instead of the patriotic Englishman, there is one who detests the thought of England. Instead of the humane lover of his kind, there is a man who cannot even think of mankind as human: Yahoos — odious beasts, not men — surround him. While he rages against man's pride he shows an arrogant pride such as few men ever have. He thinks of himself as superior to his kind, entirely superhuman in his total contempt of all men but himself. He lacks the balance that once inspired confidence in his judgment. Instead, he has become a comic and tragic figure whose every act provokes laughter and sadness, and if he wants man to adopt the ways of the noble Houyhnhnms, he will find few people ready to take him seriously.

The Lilliputian King

The king of Lilliput exemplifies pride and cruelty. He is an absolute monarch, and the features of his character which we are shown illustrate the political vices of corrupt leadership, a hunger for power, and a tyrannical attitude.

The Brobdingnagian King

Considering his very brief appearance in the story, the Brobdingnagian king is a figure well developed for the reader. The king has improved his natural gifts so well that he has become a model for princes. He first (Book II, Chapter 3) gives the appearance of great gravity and austerity (unlike the self-indulgent and pleasure-loving kings notorious all over Europe), and we discover that he is "as learned a person as any in his dominions," his education having been in "philosophy and particularly mathematics." Such a statement implies years of hard self-discipline. The king has a great deal of what is sometimes called "character," for the king's position gave him a choice of punishing himself with difficult studies or taking life lightly and enjoying himself. As a scholar, he sounds the opinions of others: he hears the opinions of "three great scholars" on what to make of Gulliver, and he is too understanding to join the three scholars in their contemptuous dismissal of Gulliver's account of himself. He realizes that this interesting little man is fragile and subject to easy destruction in Brobdingnagian surroundings. For this reason, he desires the queen to see that particular care be taken of him. And he is observant enough to have noticed the affection between Glumdalclitch and her little "pet," and he is considerate and wise enough to have her continue to care for him.

His reactions are in keeping with his education, intelligence and large nature. But in his observations, the king also shows that he has not realized that Gulliver is a *man*, whose feelings are violently harrowed by his judgments on Gulliver's native land.

Against Gulliver's incredible obtuseness, the king's virtues shine, among them the very virtues Gulliver would have him throw away merely to take on the hated and uncomfortable position of absolute tyrant. And, representing as he does the European point of view, Gulliver makes the king a measure of European man as well as of Gulliver. Western man has long since destroyed his conscience, but the Brobdingnagian king forces him to see strong principles he long ago pushed safely back into the dark hiding places of his mind.

The Houyhnhnms

The Houyhnhnms are not so much characters, but more symbolic personifications of pure reason. They are the rational, unmoved animals that man is not, and can never be. In the rationalist utopia, Houyhnhnms are an aristocratic society based on the slave labor of the bestial, almost-human Yahoos. The Houyhnhnms represent pure reason, a state which is sound in theory, but cold, comfortless, cheerless in practice. Their society has advanced to hard perfection at the expense of qualities which are essential to human survival; emotions and feelings do not enter into their controlled world. Gulliver, who would like to rise to their rarified level, finds he is unable to do so, for he is regarded as a Yahoo.

The Master Houyhnhnm

In general, the horse is calm (he quietly removes the too-familiar hand when Gulliver attempts to stroke him), intellectually curious (he examines and re-examines Gulliver), deliberate (he makes no hasty judgment on this interesting Yahoo he has found), and relatively passionless (the only passion he displays is indignation, which is "anger excited by that which is unworthy, base, or disgraceful"). His reason gives him nature as a standard (he cannot understand lying, an unnatural use of speech, nor how nature could instruct creatures to conceal what nature gave). With his devotion to nature, too, comes some difficulty of understanding what is foreign to his experience (he asks what can be the *necessity* or *use* of man's vices). The noble Houyhnhnm, however, lacks the passions that might make him a model for man's imitation, since man's struggle for goodness involves as a basic necessity the discipline and control of his passions and the use of those passions to move him to good. The horse cultivates benevolence, which in him lacks the force of human love; the horse's child or wife is no more to him than the Houyhnhnm in the farthest corner of the realm.

The Yahoos

Like the Houyhnhnms, the Yahoos are less characters than symbolic personifications. They depict the bestiality inherent in man: foul, ugly, obscene, stupid, and depraved. But Swift does not identify the odious personification of Yahoo bestiality with man himself: Gulliver does. Somewhere between this rational Heaven of Houyhnhnmism and the sensual Hell of Yahooism, Gulliver fits in. Unfortunately, he is closer to the Yahoo in physical and emotional responses than to the Houyhnhnm, and this he will not accept. Gulliver aspires to the pure reason and lofty behavior which he admires in the elite Houyhnhnms. The satiric point in this characterization is that man's misuse of reason (or his disuse of reason) *is* the reason he cannot rise much beyond the despised Yahoo.

Captain Pedro de Mendez

Captain Pedro de Mendez carries all the virtues attributed to the truly gentle man: generosity, humaneness, sensitivity, and quiet dignity. The purpose of this character is to provide sharp contrast. Swift uses this example of the good man to undercut Gulliver's black and white judgments on mankind. It is by contrast with Captain Mendez that Swift calls attention to the fact that Gulliver cannot recover his balance after the nightmare of seeing man as a Yahoo. This good captain offers Gulliver his best suit, only to have Gulliver accept just two clean shirts which will not "defile" him, for from these he can wash the Yahoo scent. It is Don Pedro who points out Gulliver's duty and tries to make him return to his people with tolerance and affection. Ironically, the obtuse Gulliver, humiliated and humbled over his banishment from the rational horse utopia, falls into the errors of misuse of reason and lack of perspective. He fails to see that he is wrong about mankind and that some men, Don Pedro for one, do possess man's greatest attribute, reason, that bit of "horse sense" that has been denied to him.

Structure

A book is built. As an architect plans a building, a writer plans a book. In a work by either kind of artist, some parts will be intended as supports for others. Some parts will exert pressure against others, some will show parallels or balances with others, and some will, by contrast or position, throw others into high relief or shadow. All these elements of structure in a good work of art will be interpoised and integrated into a recognizable unity dictated by the artist's purpose.

In mastering a book, a student will profit by examining the interrelationships of structure as a means of seeing more clearly exactly what the writer intended to do in making his book. Questions such as the following are of valuable help:

- What parts are discernible in the work?
- Do they together form a true unity?
- How is each part related to the others and to the whole structure?
- Why is a certain part placed where it is? Why is a certain episode placed near or between others?
- Does a given event or section of the book seem to have parallels elsewhere?
- Does it have contrasts elsewhere?
- What will happen to the arrangement (structure) as a whole if a certain part is taken away?
- Why is one part of the book unlike another?

Students who practise asking particular questions suggested by the guidelines above will have great advantages in seeing the structure of a work and the intentions of the author and, having seen them more clearly, will remember them better than he would otherwise.

Questions and Answers on Structure

The following questions are offered as suggestions of the kind of work that may be done on structure, and the student is warned that the answers given are by no means intended to represent *the* answer. He should exercise his own ingenuity to improve on what is given.

Question 1.

What kind of unity is discernible in *Gulliver's Travels*?

Answer

Hardly anyone can be so superficial as to think of the *Travels* as four unrelated adventure stories.

In the first place, they are presented in a *form* popular in Swift's day, the travel book — more accurately, the imaginary voyage book — and such books naturally were divided into different parts according to the countries visited. It is wise to notice that the book is not officially

Gulliver's Travels at all, but *Travels into Several Remote Nations of the World*. It has therefore the primary unity of a recognized *form* of literature.

Behind that kind of unity lies the more important unity of a *character* that grows, changes and looks back upon all his adventures as having relationships and relevance to one another, and as together tending to produce certain results: to minister to the public good by convincing men of the depravity of their conduct while at the same time holding up to them a noble model for imitation.

Thus, the second kind of unity presupposes an important third kind, which is more basic than either of the other two, the *unity of purpose*. For, before shaping a character or choosing the form of his book, the writer of such a work as this had to know why he wrote the book at all and for what end he would shape the character. The character of Gulliver, after all, serves as part of the structure of a book presumably intended to bring readers to a particular frame of mind, to a conviction, to a new way of thinking and living. There can be no doubt of what that new way of thinking and living was. It appears too often and in too many ways to be mistaken. In his postscript letter to his cousin, Sympson, Gulliver — with amusing exaggeration, of course — angrily laments the failure of his hopes: ". . . instead of seeing a full stop put to all abuses and corruptions, at least on this little island, as I had reason to expect: behold, after above six months warning, I cannot learn that my book hath produced one single effect according to may intentions . . ." In his very last sentence he confesses that unless some corruptions of his Yahoo nature had revived he would "never have attempted so absurd a project as that of reforming the Yahoo race in this kingdom."

Question 2.

Some critics have argued that there are certain flaws in the unity of *Gulliver's Travels*. Discuss.

Answer

Book III fails to exhibit a very unified structure within itself. Moreover, seen as a part in the structure of the *Travels* as a whole, it breaks off the development of the story of Gulliver.

Internally, it consists of visits to four (five if one counts Japan) separate countries, with no continuing story developing, as there was in Books I and II and as there will be in Book IV, no unity of experience for Gulliver, no continuing character or characters "playing opposite" Gulliver. Ricardo Quintana, in his *Mind and Art of Jonathan Swift*, has aptly called Book III a "catch-all for satiric fragments."

As part of the "plan" of the *Travels* as a whole, Book III brings to a sudden stop the development of themes, tone, character and even story.

It seems to be an interpolation into a story that should pass from Book II to Book IV. Gulliver ceases to be active in the events of Book III. He captures no fleets, escapes from no monkeys, is saved from no lust-maddened Yahoo-ines: he is not *involved* in what happens. He merely observes and reports. Briefly, the reader may *hope* that Gulliver and Munodi may develop a friendship and Munodi become something of a known character, but the hope quickly dies as Gulliver takes his leave for the academy at Lagado. Satirically, Book III scatters its shot over whatever Swift would like to ridicule. It does not, like Book II, persist in the development of a theme of European man's ingenious viciousness or achieve such a climactic exclamation as the Brobdingnagian king's that Gulliver's people were "the most pernicious race of little odious vermin."

Doubtless, the fact that Swift wrote Books I and II and then Book IV has much to do with the parenthetical character of Book III. Swift had already brought *Gulliver's Travels* through its climax and denouement before he began to write Book III which could be seen to be of a different nature than Books I, II, and IV.

In considering the following questions and answers on structure, the student should at all points make allowance for what has been said here about Book III, and about a point in the next paragraph below concerning Book I. But it must be remembered that Book III *is present* in the *Travels* and has to be taken into account even though it is possible to argue that Book III fits less easily into the overall structure.

Book I also shows some signs of defective structure, especially in the way Chapter 6 cuts across the development of the story. In Chapter 5, plots are thickening around Gulliver as a result of his capture of the Blefuscudian fleet, and he adds the queen to his enemies. Then, interrupting the tension, Swift outlines the utopia of Chapter 6. Aware of the awkwardness of the situation, with the utopian picture in direct contradiction to the petty vices and corruption he has been sketching, Swift attempts to correct matters by injecting the explanation that the utopian references describe the original institutions of the country and not "the most scandalous corruptions into which these people are fallen by the degenerate nature of man."

Question 3.
Why is the voyage to Lilliput placed first among the travels?

Answer
Swift's structure has to be subservient to the development of his theme and purposes. He works, in one sense, at the education of Gulliver in the ways of the world and, in another sense, towards the revelation and condemnation of man's depravity.

Gulliver is at first naïve about the world and his own nature. He must be gradually disenchanted, gradually prepared for the violent unmasking of man among the Yahoos and Houyhnhnms. Therefore, the first book presents an amusing little people who, for a time, appear harmless, inoffensive. Gulliver is not ready to grasp the horrible flaying of man he will witness in Book IV. In one sense, he is never really prepared for it. After all, the pressure of his Houyhnhnm experience was too much for his mind: it drove him mad. But in the sense considered here, Gulliver is not at first ready to accept the revelation of man's depravity. He thinks too well of his own kind. Even after discovering the treacherous cruelty of the Lilliputian court, he fails to understand its meaning very well. The discovery does not in the least turn him against man in general. In fact, so late as the second chapter of Book IV, even after the bitter outbursts in some parts of Book III, Gulliver affirms "that there were few greater lovers of mankind at that time" than himself. Book IV snaps all his previous experience into an understood pattern for him, but the previous experience had to come first.

Swift also had to consider the psychological preparation of his readers for receiving the message, for readers were no better prepared to accept Book IV than Gulliver was. Again, we must note that many readers have never become prepared for accepting Book IV. (The story of the harmless, inoffensive Lilliputians draws the reader on with its charm. The charm has been great enough to make the *Travels* a children's bedtime-story book.) The identification of Lilliputian vices and corruption with those of England, of Europe, and of man is not pressed in Book I, though the likeness is clear enough. And Gulliver's escape from having to face any serious consequences of man's pettiness allows the reader to escape facing up to the dreadful seriousness of Swift's theme. Book I amounts to light comedy when compared with the darker and grimmer insistences of Book IV and parts of Book III.

Books III and IV would not do as introductory books, and Book II's giants lack the charm of the tiny people who serve so well to introduce the reader to Gulliver's travels geographical, intellectual, emotional and moral. Book II likewise contains the violent denunciation of man as the "most pernicious race of little odious vermin that nature ever suffered to crawl upon the surface of the earth." That pill is too strong for early swallowing; a preparation for it must be made.

Question 4.

How does the structure further support the development of theme and purpose?

Answer

After the relatively mild introduction of Book I, an introduction which nevertheless shows men as petty, scheming, shockingly vicious little creatures, Swift gives us in Book II, a sudden expansion of possibilities for man and a hint of the devastating exposures that will follow. The noble Brobdingnagians are *man big*, as the sneaky Lilliputians were *man little*.

Without saying so in Book II, Swift is setting up an elevated ideal for man's imitation. Ultimately, he will suggest that this ideal can be both noble and practicable for men of good will. Simultaneously, Gulliver's own Lilliputian smallness keeps him constantly ridiculous — more ridiculous than the Lilliputians were, for among the giants Gulliver is much more helpless and subject to mishap than the Lilliputians ever were. They, at least, had fairly well mastered their environment, and when the giant man-mountain arrived, they forced him to conform to their way of life. They even molded his mind so far that he felt that he needed to defend a Lilliputian lady from the charge of carrying on an affair with him.

Book II, as we have said, foreshadows what will follow, when the Brobdingnagian king denounces men as most pernicious little odious vermin — but Gulliver rejects the king's judgment as being a consequence of narrow views and confined education. Gulliver is not ready to accept man's depravity.

Book III contains more passages of bitterness against man's corruptions than does Book II. The structure, in other words, shows a progression of anger in Gulliver, a progression of realizing man's depravity. In fact, Swift may be accused in parts of Book III of "jumping the gun" — of exhibiting a fault in the pacing of his theme here, in such passages as Gulliver's sudden and unexpected attack on political conditions in Chapter 6, his withering cynicism on man's lack of virtue, and the pride he takes in his own vices as a suitable basis for levying taxes. The fault, if it be one, is a structural fault, that of misplacing the violence and cynicism, of not saving them for their proper place in the story. That proper place would be in Book IV, *after* Gulliver identifies man with the filthy Yahoos. For it is the shock of man's likeness to Yahoos that opens the floodgates of Gulliver's wrath and abhorrence against the corruptions of his own species. The presence of these angry statements on the nature of man can possibly be explained though, if we remember that the entire tale of all four voyages is being recalled by Gulliver, in England, after his return from the land of the Houyhnhnms. In Book III, we are witness to the voice of the changed Gulliver, more so than in his restrained accounts of Lilliput and Brobdingnag.

Question 5.
What can be said of Swift's use of Gulliver as a mask?

Answer
Much more than may be suggested here. A mask is a structural device by which a writer may avoid presenting his ideas in his own

person. Gulliver speaks in his *Travels*, not Swift. Indeed, Gulliver often presents the opposite of what Swift himself would have said. Something of Gulliver as an *obtuse* mask may be seen in the Commentary on Book II, Chapter 6. He functions very often as an obtuse mask throughout the story, and at the end of Book IV he goes out still obtuse, arrogantly singing his own praises while complaining about man's pride and warning any who have the least tincture of "this absurd vice" not to "presume to appear" in his sight.

Question 6.

What can be said on the subject of plot as an element in *Gulliver's Travels*?

Answer

In the usual sense of *plot* — meaning "the series of incidents forming the skeleton of a story" and related to each other as cause and effect — there is no plot in *Gulliver's Travels*. Gulliver, for example, does not arrive in Brobdingnag *because* of anything that happened in Lilliput. Faced with such a book as the *Travels*, one must remember the suggestion in the word *plot* of *intrigue, conspiracy, planning*; for in *plotting* a book, fiction or non-fiction, a writer considers how best to arrange his materials in order to obtain the results he desires. Plot is a systematic plan to achieve a writer's purpose. Swift's plot, if you like, is against the complacency and the peace of mind of his readers. It concerns the arrangement of such materials as are discussed in the previous questions and of those to be treated in the next section of this Note.

Question 7.

Point out some effective uses of contrast as a structural device.

Answer

Book II, looking at man through one end of the telescope and seeing him as a giant, effectively contrasts man seen through the other end of the telescope as a contemptible Lilliputian. Swift contrasts man's reality with the possibilities of his greatness. Parallel contrasts are present in each book even within the character of Gulliver. He presents himself as a good-natured giant when seen against the Lilliputians, and later as a Lilliputian (morally as well as physically) against the good-natured Brobdingnagian giants. Thus, Swift very powerfully makes the point that the reader who may dismiss the pettiness and corruption of the Lilliputians as those of a little and imaginary people cannot escape when he sees his own kind of European people taking the place of the Lilliputians. Gulliver staunchly insists upon the European character of his conscience and exalts European ways of acting and thinking precisely *while* he makes his sorry appearance-by-contrast against the great Brobdingnagian.

Less obvious contrasts abound throughout the book. Two examples will have to suffice here as suggesting what may be noticed. In Book IV, when his first Yahoo seems on the point of touching him familiarly, Gulliver draws his sword (his *hanger*) and gives the brute a smart blow with the flat of it. But when the dapple gray, the intelligent and civilized horse, finds Gulliver (to him a brute Yahoo) attempting to pet him, the Houyhnhnm shakes his head, bends his brows, and *softly* raises a forefoot to remove the insulting hand. Swift thus subtly suggests who the brute in the picture is, who is given to violence and, who, on the contrary, easily controls the situation.

The second contrast is that between the generous, charitable, civilized conduct of Captain Mendez and the surly, arrogant, ungrateful manner of Gulliver at the very time Gulliver considers himself immeasurably superior to the captain. We suffer no doubts about who the gentleman in the case is, and he is *not* the recent pupil of the Houyhnhnms.

Question 8.

Show how irony in *Gulliver's Travels* becomes a structural device.

Answer

In *Gulliver's Travels*, irony becomes more than verbal. It becomes part of the entire structure of the book, so that often the meaning — and eventually the largest meaning — is seen indirectly. Observe how Swift manipulates Gulliver in Brobdingnag. When Gulliver develops a defensive contempt for things Brobdingnagian, the reader quickly sees good in the things Gulliver condemns and, conversely, evil in what he champions. Thus, Gulliver reports with contempt the Brobdingnagian preference for honest, simple, arrangements in government. He condemns the giant king's revulsion from using gunpowder to enslave his own people as "a nice, unnecessary scruple." The reader knows that Swift's opinion is quite the opposite of Gulliver's.

A similar passage occurs in the treatment of the school of political projectors in Book III. Here, Gulliver scorns all the good ideas of the projectors as "wild impossible chimaeras that never entered into the heart of man to conceive" — wild impossible chimeras like those of having kings choose their favorites for their "wisdom, capacity, and virtue" or of having ministers consult the public good!

Since the reader and Swift so clearly take leave of Gulliver in these and many similar situations, Swift's intentions must always be carefully distinguished. Gulliver must not automatically be supposed to speak for Swift. A failure to make this simple distinction has caused many a misreading of the meaning of the entire work and many a wrong-headed diatribe against Swift and his supposed misanthropy. In Book IV, should the reader suppose that, like Gulliver, Swift is moon-struck over the horses? That he is so ragingly mad about horses that for five years he has been unable to endure any human being except the horse-scented groom?

Why then suppose that Swift wants man to live like the Houyhnhnms? It is Gulliver who want that. Swift's message must be read through the irony that has become part of the structure of *Gulliver's Travels*. It must be seen obliquely, not through Gulliver's eyes. It is seen better in a moment when, with his guard down momentarily, and speaking in effect parenthetically, his pro-Houyhnhnm diatribe suspended, he refers the reader back to considering the "wise maxims in morality and government" of those least corrupted of Yahoos, the Brobdingnagians. It is only a hint that he drops, but it is enough.

Question 9.

Compare the manner of escape, rescue and return home of Gulliver from his adventures.

Answer

Swift has imparted particular significance to the ways in which Gulliver leaves the countries of his travels. One can say, in general, that there is a greater emphasis on the return as the book progresses, and as Gulliver becomes more aware of the effect that the experiences of his voyages have had upon him. At the end of Part I, he is eager to leave both Lilliput and Blefuscu, and repairs a boat on which he stores supplies for himself and the miniature cattle. He is happy to reach England, where he exhibits his curiosities for profit and thinks of his journey as little more than a novel experience.

Not so in Part II. He is physically and morally shaken when his travelling house is snatched by an eagle and dropped into the ocean. Gulliver suffers a severe upset in contemplating his doom. Even when he is rescued he cannot adjust to the size of ordinary human beings and his perspective remains distorted. He is certainly less in control of himself here than at the end of Part I. Fortunately, he finds a sympathetic and kind captain who helps him over the hurdles in re-adjusting to life and to his own kind. But Gulliver takes a long while to recover his normal sensibilities upon arriving back in his own town. The people seem to him of pygmy size, and it is only through the greatest effort of his will that he finally readjusts.

Of course, he *never* readjusts after Part IV. It is neither will nor chance which causes his departure from Houyhnhnmland, but the command of the horses. He is ostracized, banished, because he is unwanted. Gulliver rebels against returning to a society he has come to detest and, in a half-crazed state, prepares a skimpy craft which he hopes will convey him to an island on which he can live out his days in solitude. His anxiety here is much greater than anything undergone in Part II. Wounded by cannibals and in danger of being killed, he is rescued by the sailors of Pedro de Mendez, and the Portugese captain personally makes it his business to aid in Gulliver's rehabilitation. Since Gulliver is in what one would call "a state of shock," the period of recuperation takes many months. Honest, patient, understanding, Mendez is shown as a virtuous human being who does have Gulliver's interests at heart. He is the living disproof that all men are Yahoos. But even though Gulliver spends considerable time with Mendez, the former never is fully reconciled to his normal way of life. At the end of the book, Gulliver still detests Yahoo-Europeans and has become a confirmed misanthrope. Perhaps Swift has spent a particularly long time on the final return of Gulliver to show that there is not much hope of recovery for people who embrace intellectual extremes. By all rights, the sojourn with Mendez should have shown Gulliver that decent, kind, good people do exist; but failing to have seen this, Gulliver must end his days worse than a hermit — for he remains among his own kind, isolated from them and hating them.

Question 10.

While *Gulliver's Travels* is undoubtedly original, Swift drew upon several genres of writing for the composition of his book: namely, travel literature, the philosophic voyage, utopian treatises and the fable. Illustrate.

Answer

Obviously, the genre of travel literature influences the entire travels. Gulliver very definitely does travel from place to place and publishes his journals for the edification of those who have never been abroad. His scrupulous detailing of events, places, actions, etc., is also in the travel vein, since travellers, in order to appear truthful to the reader, made certain they padded their adventures with as much circumstantial detail as possible.

The elements of the philosophic voyages are present as well. In these, a traveller generally discovers peoples who are more advanced in morals, more simple in their needs than Europeans and so he is able to satirize existing institutions. Gulliver, upon becoming acquainted with the language and manners of the various countries, can dispute or argue the respective merits of them compared to Europe. Naturally, such discourse has a philosophic cast in that the glaring inadequacies of Europe are exposed.

The philosophic voyage is only a step away from utopian literature. Plato's *Republic*, Sir Thomas More's *Utopia*, Bacon's *New Atlantis* are just a few examples of imaginary societies that are perfectly ordered and governed and in which people lead full, untroubled, vital lives. Utopian elements are found in each book of the travels, but Swift makes it apparent that he is no believer in any abstract utopia. Human nature and human beings are not made to endure perfection. And if the land of the Houyhnhnms seems at first blush to be the perfect utopia, one must recall that human beings are not horses. Here, in Part IV, Swift has relied heavily on the fable, particularly as written by Aesop. This last genre is always successful for satiric purposes because the human elements can be brilliantly contrasted with the animal — which Swift does with a vengeance. Often as not, the animal emerges as superior, and human pride is whittled down a notch or two in the course of the reversal. Understanding that *Gulliver's Travels* is a book which stresses — if not preaches — moral behavior, one can conclude that Swift, like Aesop, found animals the most suitable examples from which to exhibit and draw morals for human beings.

Meaning

Curious but very common is the habit of being so engaged with the facts of a reading or with the details of chapters, of incidents, of scenes, of the mere action of a story, that the larger significance of the whole book will be missed. In such cases, perhaps the writer may be at fault, for if readers miss the meaning of a work as a whole, the writer has failed. More likely, however, if the book is one of established power and enduring quality, the reader will have to shoulder the blame when he misses the writer's message.

When a writer visits and revisits the same idea, we can assume that he is making it a theme in the book. The wise student will keep some record — brief notations, page markings, perhaps, of the places where the author touches the same subject, and will note how the subject is developing. Very probably, several themes will appear as the book progresses, and various themes will in time coalesce into one clear dominant theme which may then be considered *the* theme of the work as a whole. *Gulliver's Travels* presents a number of themes that draw together under a single dominant theme.

If the book has a plot, review the plot for hints about the total meaning. Certainly, one should expect that a book organized to carry a theme will reflect that theme in its action. If someone is seen making all his choices and living his life by the dictates of a selfish pride, what will the end of the action say by way of commentary on such a mode of living? If, in the end, his pride has brought his happiness crashing down, destroyed his family, destroyed him, the artist clearly means to say (through the action) that such a way of living is destructive of oneself, one's happiness, one's family. Presenting the action alone may be enough. Extra comment to make the point inescapable scarcely need accompany the action.

As a writer takes his farewell of his reader, as he closes what he has to say in his discussion, one may justly expect him to drop suggestions about what he wants the reader to go away thinking about. And what could be more natural than the main idea he has been working to establish? It is always well to read endings carefully and to review them. They often help to shuffle what may look like a jumble of notions into shape and unity for the reader.

No theme can be accepted merely because supporting material can be gleaned to make it look plausible. To establish the validity of a theme, we must take into account whatever conflicts with accepting it. If there are major contradictions — of plot, say — that absolutely will not fit into a scheme of thought, that scheme can scarcely be accepted as the idea the writer intended to convey.

Questions and Answers on Meaning

Question 11.

Consider some themes Swift develops in *Gulliver's Travels*.

Answer

Gulliver's Travels may seem to have a bewildering number of themes as candidates for theme-of-the-book. Very early, there emerges a theme of pride, which Swift seems determined to pound into self-abasement. Yet, even that large theme will prove subservient to another in the larger scheme of the book. Swift's constant concern with pride can be seen everywhere in the outline of the *Travels*. It appears in Bolgolam's presuming to take Gulliver as a personal enemy, in the ridiculously inflated name and the presumptuous titles of the emperor of Lilliput, in the assault on the reputations of noble families and the heroes of history (Book III), and in so many other episodes that examples seem unnecessary. Ridicule of political enemies also appears early in the book, as the Flimnap story mocks at Walpole, and Gulliver's dealings with Blefuscu become a figuring of the Tories' part in political history. The theme raises its head again and again as Gulliver reports on the gossip about Flimnap's wife, the defeat of royal measures at Lindalino, the escape of the prime minister's wife from Laputa, the destruction — by new methods — of the flourishing countryside of Balnibarbi, the means of discovering plots devised by the Lagado projectors, the brutal descriptions of prime ministers at several points, and numerous other passages.

A rather different theme intertwined with this last one is the idiocy of party rivalries seen in the *Tramecksan* and *Slamecksan*, whose real difference is one-fourteenth of an inch in the heels, or in the proposal to settle political disagreements by uniting the half-brains of political opponents. The Brobdingnag king, in circumstances that ridicule the importance of the question, mockingly asks little Grildrig whether he is a Whig or a Tory.

English jingoism frequently suffers satiric blows — from the Brobdingnagian king's contemptuous assessment of English history or the account of England as a completely irrational and unnatural country in Book IV.

In considering themes we must not overlook the one that has caused the most difficulty among Swift's critics over the years, the theme of man's animal grossness. (More accurately, the critics have been outraged by what they took to be Swift's misanthropy and his obsession with filth and man's animal functions.) Examples are: Gulliver's excremental difficulties in Lilliput and Brobdingnag, his unique method of extinguishing palace fires, his outraged description of the Brobdingnagian court maids, the filthy first projector at the Academy of Lagado, and the long-drawn presentation of the Yahoos as figures of human degradation.

Questions are persistently raised in the *Travels* about the adequacy of European values and the respectability of the European conscience. Even in Lilliput, Gulliver is abashed by the emperor's thinking it "monstrous" to "offer as a defense the greatest aggravation of the crime" of a servant's disappearing with his master's money (Gulliver had called it "only a breach of trust"). In the land of the giants, Gulliver treats the king's revulsion from the use of gunpowder as "a *nice unnecessary scruple*, whereof in Europe we can have no conception." Book III's political projectors represent attacks on what was allowed by the consciences of rules and at least accepted by European society.

In fact, when one considers the breadth of Swift's attack on the institutions of Europe, his repeated onslaughts against royal courts, lawyers, judges, justice (so called), war, government organizations and practices, king's officers, science, physicians and medicine, education, the luxury that feeds on trade, the dishonesty of European history and of the names of noble families, the falsehood of "nobility," one might think of the book as a complete and utter rejection of the corruption of European culture. Gulliver, after all, eventually prefers the chance of drowning to reuniting himself with the European Yahoo.

Question 12.

Are all the themes of the book resolved into a unity that constitutes the theme of *Gulliver's Travels*?

Answer

Yes. If the reader has not thus simplified the various strands of attack into a single theme, Gulliver does it for him at the very end of his last chapter:

> My reconcilement to the Yahoo-kind in general might not be so difficult, if they would be content with those vices and follies only which nature hath entitled them to. I am not in the least provoked at the sight of a lawyer, a pick-pocket, a colonel, a fool, a lord, a gamester, a politician, a whoremonger, a physician, an evidence, a suborner, an attorney, a traitor, or the like: this is all according to the due course of things: but when I behold a lump of deformity and diseases, both in body and mind, smitten with *pride*, it immediately breaks all the measures of my patience; neither shall I be ever able to comprehend how such an animal and such a vice could tally together. The wise and virtuous Houyhnhnms, who abound in all excellencies that can adorn a rational creature, have no name for this vice in their language, which

hath no terms to express any thing that is evil, except those
whereby they describe the detestable qualities of their
Yahoos . . . .

But the Houyhnhnms, who live under the government of
reason, are no more proud of the good qualities they possess,
than I should be for not wanting a leg or an arm, which no
man in his wits would boast of . . . .

Even in his ravings Gulliver will allow man a few vices that are
natural ("which nature entitles them to"); but it is the unnatural in
man's vices for which he has his whip out, and the chief of these is pride.
Moreover, those who live by reason are not subject to pride, even those
(the Houyhnhnms) who have most cause to be proud. Gulliver does war
on pride, but he detests it because it is monstrously unnatural and
unreasonable.

Houyhnhnmland should have made the main theme clear to the
reader. *Reason* and *nature* were the norm there, as they had been earlier
in Brobdingnag. And they were *a* norm, not two, as the Houyhnhnm's
reasoning often shows. The Houyhnhnm always automatically thinks in
terms of what is natural, the natural function or purpose, and every
departure from that is irrational. Thus, he appears baffled about how
"law, which was intended for every man's preservation, should be any
man's ruin." Departing from nature is departing from reason. He cannot rationally comprehend lying because it departs from the natural
purpose of speech. Reason serves virtue. Indeed, it is a critical passage in
which the Houyhnhnm concludes that men have not true reason but
"some quality fitted to increase our natural vices." So far has man's
alleged "reason" departed from nature that the horse cannot recognize
it as true reason.

A number of themes suggested above have the common purpose of
either exhibiting or humbling man's pride. His littleness should make
him humble, but his pretentiousness makes him ridiculous. His dignity
is in many ways a self-delusion (from abuse of reason) that loses sight of
his real position in a mighty universe. Party rivalries commonly spring
from ambition of place and power rather than from significant differences of policy. Many of the corruptions of European culture serve
vanity and the ambitions of pride, as also does the dishonesty of history,
which panders to the reputations of persons, families, or nations.

Pride itself is a departure from nature and right reason, as we have
noted. Thus, all the themes that serve the larger theme of pride will be
seen as manifestations of the still larger theme of corruption and abuse
of reason and nature. Other themes will also be found to subserve this
main larger one, those of the corruptions of law and government, which
unreasonably depart from the natural purposes for which law and
government exist, and wrong-headed science, which wastes the intellect

on foolish projects, upsets the productive working of established, successful ways, and raises irrational fears in man. The dishonesty of history and all dishonesties will appear here, for every form of lying departs from reason in perverting natural functions. So also will the deceitful inflation of man's littleness and man's self-deceiving false dignity. If European values are inadequate and European conscience corrupted, it is because they have lost sight of what nature and reason dictate as norms. These and all the minor themes of *Gulliver's Travels* unite at last to subserve the principal theme of the corruption and abuse of man's reason and of nature.

Question 13.

Is the book, then, merely negative in its final meaning? Is it merely a flaying of Swift's world for corrupting and abusing reason and nature?

Answer

Not at all. Satire must essentially keep two visions always parallel, the actual and the ideal. The actual is corrupt, but at every point its corruption suggests the ideal, man and his institutions as they should be. Thus, point for point, every condemnation of man and society suggests what can be done to remedy the situation.

But better still, Swift has presented a noble example of how man should be. If he follows that example, his institutions must naturally become what they should. In the last chapter of the *Travels* Gulliver abandons his horse-ravings long enough to drop a serious suggestion which he leaves to the *judicious* reader for "remarks and applications." Houyhnhnm-mad still, he declares that he will "say nothing [though he immediately says something] about those remote nations where Yahoos reside; amongst which the least corrupted are the Brobdingnagians, whose wise maxims in morality and government it would be our happiness to observe."

The chief representative from Brobdingnag is its admirable king, a noble model for man's imitation.

Question 14.

What effect on the meaning of the book has Gulliver's final madness?

Answer

It probably has several, but one essential effect should be noticed. The reader cannot accept the ravings of horse-mad Gulliver as Swift's serious meaning. Gulliver's final obsession is the desirability of living like the horses, a plain impossibility for man. In his asides, his departures from the main subject of his extravagance, we catch Swift's hints about what to make of *Gulliver's Travels*: go back to Brobdingnag.

The madness by no means allows us to shrug off the book with a laugh because its main message is a madman's ravings. The assault on human vice, corruption and depravity is solidly grounded. It is precisely *because* Gulliver does go mad, and is dissociated from Swift, that the message of the book has to be taken seriously.

Question 15.
Does any evidence *outside* the book have a bearing on its meaning?

Answer
Evidence outside a book should always be used cautiously in establishing meaning. What a writer says at the age of 25 may or may not be relevant to what he means 40 years later, when experience has presumably matured his attitudes and opinions.

There are, however, several letters relevant to our problem because Swift wrote them at the time of *Gulliver's Travels* and wrote them *about* the book. Was Swift, as some critics have chosen to insist, a raving misanthrope demonstrating total hatred of his species? *Gulliver's Travels* itself will not support such an opinion. Neither will the letters.

To his friend, Charles Ford, who later served Swift well as a go-between with printers, Swift wrote on August 14, 1725, "I have finished my Travels, and I am now transcribing them; they are admirable things, and will wonderfully mend the World." He wrote, at least partly tongue-in-cheek, no doubt, but the tone is positive. Less than a a month later, September 11, 1725, he wrote to another friend, Thomas Sheridan, who had fallen out of favor with the men of power in Ireland, ". . . sit down and be quiet, and mind your own business as you should do, and contract your friendships and expect no more from man than such an animal is capable of, and you will every day find my description of Yahoos more resembling." — Or, Gulliver was right! In the same month, on September 29, he wrote to Alexander Pope that he had been spending his time in

> . . . finishing, correcting, amending, and transcribing my Travels, in four parts complete, newly augmented, and intended for the press, when the world shall deserve them, or rather when a printer shall be found brave enough to venture his ears . . . .

> . . . the chief and I propose to myself in all my labours is to vex the world rather than divert it; and if I could compass that design, without hurting my own person or fortune, I would be the most indefatigable writer you have ever seen without reading . . . when you think of the world give it one lash the more at my request. I have ever hated all na-

tions, professions, and communities, and all my love is toward individuals: for instance, I hate the tribe of lawyers, but I love Counsellor Such-a-one, and Judge Such-a-one: so with physicians — I will not speak of my own trade — soldiers, English, Scotch, French, and the rest. But principally I hate and detest that animal called man, although I heartily love John, Peter, Thomas, and so forth. This is the system upon which I have governed myself many years, but do not tell, and so I shall go on till I have done with them. I have got materials toward a treatise, proving the falsity of that definition *animal rationale*, and to show it would be only *rationis capax*. Upon this great foundation of misanthropy, though not in Timon's manner, the whole building of my Travels is erected; and I never will have peace of mind till all honest men are of my opinion. By consequence you are to embrace it immediately, and procure that all who deserve my esteem may do so too.

Mr. Lewis sent me an account of Dr. Arbuthnot's illness, which is a very sensible affliction to me, who, by living so long out of the world, have lost that hardness of heart contracted by years and general conversation. I am daily losing friends, and neither seeking nor getting others. Oh! if the world had but a dozen Arbuthnots in it, I would burn my Travels. But, however, he is not without fault ... our Doctor has every quality and virtue that can make a man amiable or useful; but, alas! he has a sort of slouch in his walk.

Swift often engaged in such playful bullying of his friends as he does here in his peremptory *order* that Pope immediately embrace Swift's opinion of man. Swift should not be read as literally meaning everything he says. But on the subject of misanthropy, Swift insists that he hates men in masses but loves them as individuals. His misanthropy hardly deserves the name at all. As no misanthrope would, he speaks of "all honest men" and "all who deserve my esteem." And the illness of his friend, Dr. Arbuthnot (a Scotsman and a physician), is to Swift what it would not be to any misanthrope, "a very sensible affliction" because he lacks the hardness of heart he might have had if his life had been spent more in society. (A misanthrope has no friends.)

Two months later (November 26), he again wrote to Pope. "Drown the world!" he exclaims. "I am not content with despising it, but I would anger it, if I could with safety." Pope and all his friends, he hopes, will take care not to impute his "disaffection to the world to his age." From the age of 21, he declares, his opinion has not changed. "I tell you, after all, that:

I do not hate mankind: it is *vous autres* (you others) who hate them, because you would have them reasonable animals, and are angry for being disappointed. I have always rejected that definition, and made another of my own. I am no more angry with _____ than I was with the kite that last week flew away with one of my chickens; and yet I was pleased when one of my servants shot him two days after.

Question 16.

No one country that Gulliver visits is considered by Swift to be an ideal utopia, yet utopian elements are found in each of them. What are some from each country?

Answer

While the Lilliputians would seem to have little to commend them, Swift does not detract from their institutions entirely. Some of their laws and customs could certainly be incorporated into any body of government with excellent results. In Lilliput — before it grew decadent — false accusers were punished more severely than those guilty of crime; fraud was considered a greater crime than theft; any who had led a blameless life were rewarded by the government; people were chosen for government posts because they possessed superior morals and virtues as well as intelligence; ingratitude was a capital crime; communal nurseries were limited in size so that children might get a superior education as early as possible, etc. All in all, the older institutions of Lilliput are to be envied.

The Brobdingnagians, too, have many ideal customs, laws and procedures. The wiles of political intrigue have been reduced to a minimum. Morality, poetry, history and mathematics are emphasized in the schools, and the latter is directed to making practical advances in art and agriculture. The standing army is composed of volunteers — and all men volunteer since wars are almost non-existent in a kingdom ruled by a benevolent and gracious king who is interested only in the welfare of his people.

Difficult as it may be in Part III to find any enduring utopian principles, a few can be isolated. The Laputans control scientific information which could be potentially valuable to mankind, although they as yet are too short-sighted to understand its value. Learning is means and end to the Laputans, something not despicable in itself but weakened by the impracticality of the uses to which learning is put. Becoming cognizant of human wants, the Laputans could do many great things with their knowledge. In Gulliver's voyage to Luggnagg, he discovers a people courteous and kind, and philosophically composed to accept death in view of the omnipresent Struldbruggs who provide living examples of the vanity and horror of immortality.

But perhaps the society of Part IV offers some of the most desirable bases for a utopia. The "grand maxim" of the Houyhnhnms is to "cultivate reason and to be wholly governed by it," and the two principal virtues they possess are friendship and benevolence. They never lie. Indeed, they have no name for lying in their language; they practise birth control so that their land can support its inhabitants. The youth are brought up to be continent and stoic, and are taught temperance, industry, exercise and cleanliness. Lastly, the Houyhnhnms live basically simple lives, "wasting not and wanting not," and greeting death without fear or pain.

Question 17.

What aspects of monarchy (positive and negative) does Swift attempt to portray in each book?

Answer

The corrupt, court-centered world of Lilliput brings out what is generally the worst in all monarchies. Backbiting, chicanery, political juggling, deceit, treachery, vindictiveness — the stock-in-trade of courtiers — is here exercised most flagrantly. The vying for favors and attention and knightly orders are further indications of the decadence into which the monarchy has fallen. Again, the double-talk and blatant exaggeration of government decrees — like the list of charges drawn up against Gulliver — indicate the perversions a tyrant can exercise in order to accomplish his ends.

At the other pole is Brobdingnag. Here, the king rules through love, not fear. He is kind, benevolent, gracious, always seeking the well-being of his subjects. It might justly be said, however, that he is somewhat too naïve to ever make a truly strong king. Brobdingnag is isolated from the rest of the world, and therefore the king can remain aloof from problems facing monarchies bounded on all sides. It is hard to imagine a ruler remaining philosophic in the midst of wars and revolutions: occasions rather remote under the circumstances.

The easy, open, relaxed, unpretentious atmosphere about the court in Brobdingnag is contrasted sharply to the kingdom of Laputa, where the ruler is even more tyrannical than the Lilliputian monarch. Potentially more dangerous than the little emperor because he possesses dangerous weapons with which to intimidate his subjects, the Laputan king is only prevented from embarking on a reign of terror by his preoccupation with more abstract things. This, of course, is both beneficial and detrimental. Owing to impractical and shoddy governing, the country has fallen into decay. The lands are blasted and wasted and revolution is fomenting constantly. All in all, there is really little virtue in a kingdom which does not direct its energy toward caring for its people.

The kingdom in Part IV presents an interesting problem since it may hardly be considered a monarchy at all. The Houyhnhnms seem to have a kind of limited dictatorship, though their general assembly bears close affinities with the English parliament. Quasi-fascistic, quasi-democratic, the country hardly has any one type of rule at all. To be sure, the Yahoos are oppressed and kept in the subservient position of slaves, but at the same time Houyhnhnmland approaches something like the Greek city-states. Thus, while principles of monarchy are not exclusively operating here, there are elements. The grand assembly is composed of the patriarch horses and these arbitrarily made the decisions. With monarchy, then, a paradoxically tyrannical and liberal spirit is operating simultaneously. But there has never been anything simple about Part IV of the travels.

Question 18.

"The chief function of reason, according to eighteenth-century views, was to fit a man for a happy life among his fellows." Does *Gulliver's Travels* always agree with this philosophy?

Answer

There are times throughout the travels when it seems certain that Gulliver will come to his senses and let reason dictate his course of life. It is reason which compels Gulliver to have nothing to do with his hypocritical medical brethren and ship to sea in search of a more honest, conscience-liberating livelihood. Thus, Gulliver, at the beginning, shuns a career that would make him morally unsound and ultimately unhappy. His experiences in Lilliput open his eyes to the cant, cunning and corruption of the world, and one might imagine that Gulliver will prove himself above these faults. Not so, however. He proves himself something of a worm in Part II when he tries to hoodwink the king of Brobdingnag. His wit and reason sharpened, Gulliver becomes as petty as the Lilliputians and grows almost blind to the unhappy course he is charting for himself. Certainly, Part III shows Gulliver ill-equipped to remain happy in a society where reason has been perverted. Man remains slave to the machine and mathematics replaces emotions.

Though Gulliver learns at last to embrace reason untainted by passion or abstraction, he becomes as miserable as anyone could. He is unable to face his fellows on his return from Houyhnhnmland, and growls misanthropic curses and imprecations at all with whom he comes into contact. One can see from *Gulliver's Travels* that Swift was being terribly cautious about the power of reason. Merely possessing it was not, for him, the formula for being a reasonable human being. It was not man's having reason, but his employing it, that became the final test for Swift. And so, while some men could possess a superabundance of reason, life was not made easier or happier because of it. The individual conscience and intelligence, common sense and moral wholeness dictated as much, if not more, than any storehouse of reason. Like most things, the *quality* of the possession, not the *quantity*, dictates true happiness.

Question 19.
Why might Swift have chosen horses to rule Houyhnhnmland?

Answer
To have animals governing utopian lands was not original with Swift, but it can be supposed that he chose horses for several good reasons when it came to constructing his own treatment of utopia. First, in order to shame the reader into realizing how imperfect he is, Swift must contrast the human being with something else not remotely human. Thus, the horse. It is quasi-domestic and not that foreign to the majority of people; it is quasi-wild and thereby becomes removed from domestic institutions. In either case, the horse can be imagined as something magnificent, fast, graceful, preserving its nobility in any situation. Horses have, in fact, always been associated through history and myth with the aristocracy or royalty of one sort or another. Indeed, rulers are often remembered for their horses rather than for the people they ruled. Horses, too, give the appearance of being less fawning or servile than other domestic animals, and they convey a sense of power and force that one can not easily imagine in dogs, sheep, cows, or cats. It is equally important that horses have been considered through the ages to possess what is idiomatically known as "horse sense." Whether or not these animals are really endowed with it makes little difference. The myth has been built up around the supposition that they have, and so Swift has manipulated it for his own purposes.

Style

It is easy enough to give a definition of style. Style is "the manner of expressing oneself in language," or perhaps — if the desire is to speak of a given writer's style — "the manner of expressing himself that is characteristic and distinctive of that writer." Jonathan Swift defined style as "proper words in proper places," a definition we shall revisit and one that seems to demand a meeting of judgments in the writer and the critic.

But having given a definition, one must also look into the Pandora's box of which it is the lid. For so many and such subtle elements enter into style that one can hardly speak of style *in general* at all. Something may be said of a particular style, of a given writer's style. In this sense, we must understand the well-known declaration that "style is the man." Yet, the statement is inadequate, for a man's style changes to suit the necessities of what he is trying to say. Style is rather the man's expression under a given necessity. Romeo's loving goodnight to Juliet:

> Sleep dwell upon thine eyes, peace in thy breast!
> Would I were sleep and peace, so sweet to rest!

has Shakespeare's mystery of language, but the tone of the lines, their gentleness and love-languishing feeling, contrasts with the harsh

> Tybalt, you rat-catcher, will you walk?

— yet both passages appear in the same play. Whatever may be said of a man's style in general, the great writer must be versatile in fitting his style to the necessities of the particular occasion. And he will do it so smoothly, so inconspicuously that unless the reader makes an effort he will not notice what is happening, for true art conceals the artifice that makes it great.

To understand a style, the student does well to ask in every conceivable way *how* a writer presents his meaning. Some useful questions (of possible hundreds) the reader may propose to himself will be suggested here.

What general impression does the passage or work convey to the reader? *How* in general does the man write? Is the style

- fitted to the material or at odds with it?
- clear in presenting the thought — or muddy?
- redundant (wordy) or concise?
- formal? or colloquial, chatty, personal? journalistic?
- stiff, or easy and familiar?
- monotonous or varied?
- interesting or dull?

- slow-moving or rapid in development?
- abstract or concrete?
- unobtrusive, or distracting the reader from what is said?
- logical? emotional? mixed?
- persuasive, or unconvincing?
- straightforward or given to figurative language?
- fresh, or staled by trite expressions?
- true to one point of view or shifting from one to another?

How would one characterize the writer's diction (his choice of words)? Are his words

- simple (natural) or pedantic or affected?
- colloquial, slangy, dialectal, archaic, obsolete, technical, standard?
- accurately chosen or imprecise?
- monosyllabic or employing a mature vocabulary?
- abstract or concrete?
- ordinary or given to the unusual, to pomposity and fanciness?
- inflated by jargon?

How does the writer construct his sentences? Are his sentences

- monotonous, or varied in structure? in length?
- smooth, or given to awkwardness (awkward passives, awkward repetitions)?
- well co-ordinated or choppy?
- loose or periodic?
- full of tension, or flabby?
- normal in word order or prone to unusual variations?
- carefully arranged to secure proper coordination and subordination of ideas?
- grammatical or ungrammatical?
- rhythmic, or jerky and unbalanced?

How does he organize his paragraphs?

- With a care for unity? Do his paragraphs revolve around a clear central idea?
- With the smoothness that follows effective transitional devices between the inside sentences? Do gaps in thought occur?
- With a fair regularity of length, or with significant variations?
- With logical strength or illogical weakness?
- With reliance on logic or on emotion?
- With the weakness of undeveloped generalities or with the clarity and strength of specific details?

— With clear connections between neighboring paragraphs and binding transitions among them?

This is a start on what to examine for in style. But the list might continue indefinitely. In the end, a *good* style will show clear organization of the entire book and succeed in presenting the author's purpose. Thus, style is related to *structure*.

Questions and Answers on Style

Question 20.

How, in general, would you characterize the style of *Gulliver's Travels*?

Answer

Its style is protean (shifting, changing), varying to suit the special purpose Swift seeks to achieve. It is especially complicated by Swift's versatile use of irony (see the following question). He is not a writer with a fixed and steady literary personality whose style may be characterized once and for all.

Nevertheless, some observations may be made that apply to his style whether he happens to be calm or explosive. His diction will always be simple, in accordance with his own advice "To a Young Gentlemen Lately Entered into Holy Orders." Though his remarks slant towards pulpit oratory, the subject is *style*. Too many clergymen, he says, neglect the fundamental necessity of studying the English language, with the result that they speak in "a flat Kind of Phraseology, often mingled with barbarous Terms and Expression." The true definition of style he gives as "proper words in proper places;" and the search for proper words will avoid "obscure Terms, also called *hard words* and *fine language*." He has, he says, listed "several hundred Words in a Sermon of a new Beginner, which not one of his Hearers among a Hundred could possibly understand;" and he recommends a test he has heard Lord Falkland used for selecting and rejecting words: try them out on the chambermaid. If she understands them, use them.

> A common Farmer shall make you understand in three words that his Foot is out of Joint, or his Collar-bone broken; wherein a Surgeon, after a hundred Terms of Art, if you are not a Scholar, shall leave you to seek. It is frequently the same Case in Law, Physick, and even many of the meaner Arts.

He lists words he doubts are proper to use before ordinary congregations:

I defy the greatest Divine, to produce any Law either of God or Man which obliges me to comprehend the meaning of Omniscience, Omnipresence, Ubiquity, Attribute, Beatific Vision, with a Thousand others so frequent in Pulpits; any more than that of Excentrick, Idiosyncracy, Entity, and the like . . .

. . . a Divine hath nothing to say to the wisest Congregation of any Parish in this Kingdom, which he may not express in a Manner to be understood by the meanest among them.

If Swift recommended the language of the people for Sunday sermons, he used the same language of the people for his Gulliverian sermon to the world.

Swift will always be concise, which does not mean that he will always force his thought into the absolutely fewest possible words, but that he steadfastly sticks to the point, realizes when *enough has been said* to drive home his point, and leaves it as soon as that much has been said. Perhaps we may call this conciseness "having a rigorous concern for making his point." Herbert Davis, a leading contemporary Swift scholar, treats this conciseness well in his *Jonathan Swift, Essays on His Satire and Other Studies* (see particularly pp. 217-218). Of Swift's devotion to making his point Davis says, "He never deviated from this particular purpose, never allowed himself to hesitate, to make qualifications or concessions." Davis doubts that Swift's style can be detected by "any particular mannerism or tricks of phrase . . . His style is never mannered." Nor, thinks Davis, can it be identified even by "a certain biting humour or of irony." But it can be identified by the conciseness we have spoken of. In two ways simplicity is a leading mark of all Swift's writing: simplicity of diction and simplicty of intention (sticking to the point so long as it remains the point and not complicating things by intermixing other points).

But let us consider more particularly the style Swift devised for Gulliver. It is, we have said, protean. The opening of the book shows a style well-adapted to Swift's purpose. Gulliver speaks in a low key of the merest matters of fact, his own perfectly ordinary and undistinguished history. There is no excitement as he opens his story:

My father had a small estate in Nottinghamshire; I was the third of five sons. He sent me to Emanuel College in Cambridge at fourteen years old, where I resided three years and applied myself close to my studies . . . .

Here he uses a plain, unsophisticated narrative style that employs the vocabulary of an ordinary Englishman totally uninterested in anything except delivering simple truth in simple terms. There is no pretentiousness in such language as he uses: "Some of them attempted with spears to stick me in the sides" or ". . . I walked near a mile before got to the shore." Some of his expressions, like his saying he "was bound apprentice" or that his effort to establish a practice among the sailors at Wapping "would not turn to account," though possibly unfamiliar to readers' ears today, were familiar enough in Swift's time; they help to establish his character as a usual kind of Englishman with the vocabulary of the class of people who have to earn a living.

The book about Lilliput opens with a slow, plodding, common place style very like that of the stories of Daniel Defoe (*Robinson Crusoe*, etc.). This serves a very necessary end, that of establishing our confidence in Gulliver as one who may be believed because he is one of "ourselves" and yet has the experience and training to recommend his reports to our attention. Swift also, as we observed in tracing the story of Book I, wishes to secure verisimilitude, to make the imaginary lands seem a part of the real world. Style serves this purpose. Receiving from Gulliver an account of mere matters of fact, the reader suddenly finds among the facts a land of tiny people. Lulled by a style intentionally unexciting, slow-moving, the unwary reader suddenly realizes that he has arrived in a land of wonders. He has, as it were, slept his way from Nottinghamshire to Lilliput. It fits the style marvelously that Gulliver sleeps his way into Mildendo. His so sleeping, indeed, should be considered a device of style, part of how Swift presents his story.

Different conditions and different purposes will bring changes in Swift's style. How unlike the opening of the *Travels* is its close, where the pages are electric with the charge of Gulliver's emotional state. On European "colonization" he writes:

> . . . Here commences a new dominion acquired with title by *divine right*. Ships are sent with the first opportunity; the natives driven out or destroyed, their princes tortured to discover their gold; a free license given to all acts of inhumanity and lust; the earth reeking with the blood of its inhabitants; and this execrable crew of butchers employed in so pious an expedition, is a *modern colony* sent to convert and civilize an idolatrous and barbarous people.

Tone is the great difference between this and the last-considered passage. Here, Swift has an edge of bitterest sarcasm on his irony instead of the straightforward delivery of facts previously observed. The style abounds in exciting images and epithets: natives driven out or destroyed. . . princes tortured. . . gold. . . license to all acts of inhumanity and lust. . . execreable crew of butchers. . . earth reeking with blood.

As it always is, Swift's diction here is distinguished because he realized his own ideal of proper words in proper places. In this passage

is safe to say, proper words for Swift were not *unusual* words. His
vocabulary is precise rather than extraordinary. Aside from the few
words no longer used as they were in his day (*splenetics, an evidence,
discoverers*), the Gulliver vocabulary will not send to the dictionary any
reader with a normal acquaintance with English. As if Swift would
prove the rule by the exception, we observe that when he reaches for the
unusual word he does so to make it the instrument of a comic effect.
When he names (Book III, Chapter 6) the remedies to be administered
to the parliament members on the fourth day of every session, he shows
typical Swiftian exuberance of fun. The very heaping up of *hard words*
is the fun. Physicians will administer to each senator

> ... lenitives, aperitives, abstersives, corrosives, restringents,
> palliative, laxatives, cephalalgics, icterics, apophlegmatics,
> acoustics, as their several cases required ....

Dr. John Arbuthnot called *Gulliver's Travels* a merry book. Too many
readers have missed its merriment.

If one examines the individual sentences of a paragraph of Swift's,
he may conclude that the manner is ordinary:

> My gentleness and good behaviour had gained so far on the
> Emperor and his court, and indeed upon the army and
> people in general, that I began to conceive hopes of getting
> my liberty in a short time.

The sentence is a straightforward march to meaning. It shows no
ornament, no peculiarities of expression or structure. But in its *order* it
manages a nice tension, a suspension of meaning from its beginning to
its end. The proper words are in their proper places. Note how the
sentence would collapse if it were re-organized to betray the main
concern of Gulliver at the start:

> (I began to hope to get my liberty in a short time, because my
> gentleness and good behaviour had gained so far on the
> Emperor and his court, and indeed upon the army and
> people in general.)
> I took all possible methods to cultivate this favourable dis-
> position. The natives came by degrees to be less apprehen-
> sive of any danger from me. I would sometimes lie down, and
> let five or six of them dance on my hand. And at last the boys
> and girls would venture to come and play at hide and seek in
> my hair. I had now made a good progress in understanding
> and speaking their language.

With one exception, these sentences begin with the subject. They are all monotonously alike in their length and cadence. They are a simple declarative sentences. One might like to see some clear transitio between the two last sentences and a clear indication of how the la sentence fits into the development of the paragraph. His progress in t language, we are forced to infer, must be one of Gulliver's methods cultivate the favorable disposition, but Swift makes us work hard for t connection.

> The Emperor had a mind one day to entertain me with
> several of the country shows, wherein they exceed all nations
> I have known, both for dexterity and magnificence.

Here, the monotony is broken by a longer and more complicate structure, its parts neatly subordinated to secure a smooth-runnir sentence. In "both for dexterity and magnificence" the parallelism imperfect.

> I was diverted with none so much as that of the rope-dancers,
> performed upon a slender white thread, extended about two
> foot, and twelve inches from the ground.

"Extended about two foot," a colloquialism, keeps Gullive among his people. The sentence is apt to catch the reader in a momer tary ambiguity with "extended about two foot, and twelve inches fro the ground." The comma saves the situation.

> Upon which I shall desire liberty, with the reader's patience,
> to enlarge a little.

Gulliver gives us simultaneously both a fragment and a pronour reference error. We should, however, be curious about why he wishes t enlarge upon the *ground*. The fragment does manage the tension of near-periodic structure.

The passage examined belongs to that early part of the book in whic Gulliver's character as an ordinary good fellow of an Englishman has t be presented and preserved. Whether these observations are typical c Swift's sentences and paragraphs in the book as a whole the student i encouraged to decide by examining passages from other parts of th *Travels*. The sentences can by no means be called brilliant. Othe qualities than the perfection of its sentences must account for the succes of the book.

Swift's paragraphs vary in length. A random thumbing of the boo will show any number of three-line paragraphs and any number of lon ones. At the opening of Book I, four paragraphs of either ordinary o short length precede a fifth that extends for *six pages*. Then, all in on enormous paragraph, Swift transports the reader from Bristol through months of a long voyage, a shipwreck, a landing on a strange island, two long sleeps, an awakening in captivity, efforts to escape, submission to a tiny people, a large meal offered in small portions, a parley with a royal messenger, and a long, slow progress (while Gulliver sleeps on a low wagon) to the capital city of Mildendo. Such a paragraph simply can not be forced into unity by one topic sentence, and the difficulty is the greater because of the detail in which some of the events are described. Readers doubtless fail to notice the sprawling monstrosity of the paragraph because the story charms them so much that they do not require the relief of a paragraph ending.

Question 21.

How does Swift's irony complicate the style?

Answer

Irony necessarily complicates style, being a very important part of the *manner* in which the writer delivers his thoughts. Irony presents meaning by indirection — the style is that of saying what one does *not* mean, but simultaneously letting the reader somehow know what *is* meant. Besides commanding many forms of irony, Swift does not hesitate to switch from one to another, changing the style and sometimes trapping the reader who has not been quick to note the difference in the irony.

In Chapter 5 of Book III, Swift describes a project of the mathematical school at Lagado whereby pupils were to learn "after a method scarce imaginable to us in Europe."

> The proposition and demonstration were fairly written on a thin wafer, with ink composed of a cephalic tincture. This the student was to swallow upon a fasting stomach, and for three days following eat nothing but bread and water. As the water digested, the tincture mounted to his brain, bearing the proposition along with it. But the success hath not hitherto been answerable, partly by some error in the *quantum* or composition, and partly by the perverseness of lads, to whom this bolus is so nauseous, that they generally steal aside, and discharge it upwards before it can operate; neither have they been yet persuaded to use so long an abstinence as the prescription requires.

This type of irony neither praises nor blames the subject described. It is an apparently non-committal sort of irony. The speaker supposedly passes no judgment on values, and the reader must pick up the unspoken meaning from the total ridiculousness of the project itself or from an already established general attitude of the speaker. The *reportorial* tone of this irony sets up an attitude. It is a *style* of delivering the writer's material. And, if it suddenly changes, the reader has been "set up" for a surprise.

Swift's next paragraph does bring surprise and change. The irony suddenly turns to a *blame-praise irony* that depends upon the reader to know that what the speaker blames, the writer intends to praise.

> In the school of political projectors I was but ill entertained, the professors appearing in my judgment wholly out of their senses, which is a scene that never fails to make me melancholy. These unhappy people were proposing schemes for persuading monarchs to choose favourites upon the score of their wisdom, capacity, and virtue; of teaching ministers to consult the public good; of rewarding merit, great abilities, eminent services; of instructing princes to know their true interest by placing it on the same foundation with that of their people; of choosing for employments persons qualified to exercise them; with many other wild impossible chimaeras, that never entered before into the heart of man to conceive; and confirmed in me the old observation, that there is nothing so extravagant and irrational which some philosophers have not maintained for truth.

The entire tone of the passage, the whole style, differs from that of the preceding paragraph. Gulliver is suddenly savage, not mild; suddenly a violent rejecter, not a reporter, of what he sees. But the material itself (that government be wise, able, honest, etc.) speaks for what the satirist would commend. What he really condemns is the vicious absence of good government in Europe, and the fact that even proposing such a government would be a "wild impossible chimaera" beyond all imagining. One commentator has been trapped by the change in irony into calling it "a slip in Swift's satiric technique" and saying that it is "inconsistent with his satiric technique to show these political projectors to be on the sensible side of things." Swift's satiric technique is amazingly versatile and variable. A reader is wrong if he expects to limit Swift to one method alone.

In fact, the technique immediately shifts in the paragraph following this example of blame-praise irony. Gulliver declares he will do the justice to say that not all the political projectors were so visionary. One "illustrious person had very usefully employed his studies" to understand the parallel between the natural and the political bodies, with the result that he would cure political diseases on the fourth day of a senate's meeting by having physicians administer "lenitives, aperitives, abstersives, corrosives, restringents," etc. The same "illustrious person" also offered the "wonderful contrivance" of curing political disagreements by selecting the leaders of two opposing parties and matching them up two by two according to the size of their heads.

> .. then let two nice operators saw off the occiput of each couple at the same time, in such a manner that the brain may be equally divided. Let the occiputs thus cut off be interchanged, applying each to the head of his opposite party-man.

In this twist of style, the irony is called *praise-blame*, the speaker supposedly approving the suggestions of this "illustrious person." Certainly, Swift intends another meaning than Gulliver's to be understood.

Sometimes the irony is situational. Then it affects the style by depending on the surrounding circumstances to reveal the true meaning despite the speaker's intention. On the return voyage from Houyhnhnmland, Gulliver speaks of Captain Mendez as "a very courteous and generous person," offers some examples of the captain's hospitable attentions, and declares that he "wondered to find such civilities from a Yahoo. However, I remained silent and sullen; I was ready to faint at the very smell of him and his men." Captain Mendez continued his humane treatment despite Gulliver's crude rudenes and "spoke so very movingly," Gulliver says, "that at last I descended to treat him like an animal which had some little portion of reason."

The situation of contrast between the men, with Gulliver obviously acting the Yahoo boor while holding himself in a falsely superior position, produces the irony that gives the lie to Gulliver's opinions and to his assumption of superiority. Men are not Yahoos, if Mendez is an example. And that Gulliver is capable of acting, thinking and speaking as he does at the very time he delivers so glowing an account of this paragon of a captain, Mendez proves that Gulliver's judgment is no longer reliable or sound in the least. We can no longer subscribe to what he says, as we formerly could when he was a solid, judicious, honest Englishman.

We have considered four ways in which irony complicates the style of *Gulliver's Travels*. There are other ways which would be fruitful to pursue.

Question 22.

What significant and imaginative etymologies might be provided for the following names: Gulliver, Lilliput, Brobdingnag, Laputa, Houyhnhnm, Yahoo?

Answer

Swift's neologisms — i.e., coined words or names — relate in several instances to actual etymologies, or at least reasonably conjectured ones. The name "Gulliver" — perhaps the most fitting designation for a hero anywhere — is undoubtedly allied to "gullible," which is what he proves to be throughout the greater part of his travels, and relates even more severely to "gull," one able to be easily tricked or deceived. "Lilliput," a word that has passed into our language since *Gulliver's Travels*, seems less certain in origin. A most reasonable assumption is that "lill" is a contraction of "little;" and linked with "put," a rustic fellow or stranger. Only the most wild conjecture will serve for "Brobdingnag," and it might be well just to take it at face value — a gigantic, almost unpronounceable word that accords well with the oversized people of the country. "Laputa" has a vaguely Spanish sound and might derive mostly from "puta," a prostitute, indicating that the people of the Flying Island have prostituted their learning and intelligence for fly-by-night, crackpot schemes. "Puta" might be again associated with "Lilliput," therefore changing the etymology rather drastically and making the meaning more bitter; instead of "little strangers," we get "little corrupted ones," which serves as well, if not better. Two of the more ingenious names devised by Swift are found in Part IV. "Houyhnhnm" attempts to capture almost phonetically the whinny of a horse and at the same time communicate the difficulty of the language (as Gulliver himself observes). "Yahoo," of course, is a wild, raucous, uncontrolled animal sound made by uncouth or rowdy people. "Yah" — one of the roots — is itself an expression of contempt, disgust and derision. Swift has nicely contrasted the gentle, suggestive language and personality of the horse, the crude and incontinent character of the Yahoos in their respective names.

Question 23.
Summarize the main devices of rhetorical irony Swift employs.

Answer
Swift's overall ironic effect is achieved through employing the *persona* (or *mask*) — in this case the naïve hero, Gulliver. Gulliver's straight-faced recounting of adventures, his blind credulity, his obtuseness, his stubborness in sticking to appearances while the reader grasps at once the realities, all contribute to setting the ironic pattern. Again, Swift employs the rhetorical device of *litotes* (or *understatement*), the irony which makes something more important by apparently diminishing or underplaying it. For example, after Gulliver has resided in Lilliput for some time and seen the blatant intrigue and chicanery going on in court circles, he can naïvely conclude when Flimnap and Bolgolam go in league against him that "this was the first time I began to conceive some imperfect ideas of courts and ministers." Yet another ironic device is *invective*, the direct condemnation of a subject through a

series of violent and bitter epithets, seen in the travels in the concluding words of the Brobdingnagian king to Gulliver and in Gulliver's own catalogues of ills of the human race to the Master Houyhnhnm. *Sarcasm*, a display of contempt concealed under praise is found in Part III when, in viewing the Academy of Lagado, Gulliver exhibits his adulation for the lame-brained scientific schemes while Swift is all the while sneering. Lastly, the device of *ridicule*, that is, making large things small and mean, is best related to Parts I and II. Part I ridicules the pettiness and follies of humanity by making it small and mean, and Part II achieves the same effect through a reverse method.

Review of Criticism

The sanest and soundest criticism of *Gulliver's Travels* has evolved since Charles Whibley delivered the Leslie Stephen Lecture of 1917 on Jonathan Swift. Since that time, commentators have been more willing than before both to examine the work as a literary composition and to base their judgments on the *book itself* rather than on their estimates of Swift's character. Though the book received an enthusiastic and admiring welcome when it appeared, in years following it was too often regarded as an expression of Swift's personality, and both the book and the personality were outrageously and sometimes maliciously misinterpreted.

John Boyle, Fifth Earl of Orrery

Orrery defines the *Travels* as "a moral political romance, in which Swift seems to have exerted the strongest efforts of a fine irregular genius," and again as "an irregular essay of Swift's peculiar wit and humour." Though he finds the wit and the imagination delightful, Orrery declares that "the venomous strokes of his satyr, although in some places just, are carried into so universal a severity, that not only all human actions, but human nature itself, is placed in the worst light." The shining attributes of men like Newton and Bacon ("not to mention Boyle") were certainly known to Swift; but he had been, through disappointment, made "splenetic and angry with the whole world." Gulliver tires readers with pointless dwelling upon the exact proportions of sizes in Books I and II; these "amazing discoveries" should have been developed to produce improvement as well as astonishment. Orrery objects to Swift's often showing "an indelicacy that is not agreeable" and using his wit to glance at religion. He finds Swift too eager to seize any opportunity of "debasing and ridiculing his own species." Quite off the critical track, Orrery turns to marvel at the ways of Providence in having this mighty wit and genius live into a mental decay that punished his own pride and terrifies ours, and he produces two letters describing the horrors of Swift's latter years. He finds the Brobdingnag and Lilliput narrative "very entertaining and ridiculous" where it is free from "indelicacies."

Generally speaking, Orrery applauds the satiric purposes of Book III, but he piously shrinks away from the "filth" and "descriptions that shock our delicacy" in Chapter 6. The voyage to Laputa appears to him to have been rushed to a finish carelessly. Especially disappointing, he thinks, is the failure to develop the possibilities of Glubbdubbdrib, where Gulliver had the opportunity to call up whom he pleased from the dead. Swift wastes his chance on trifles like the cause of Alexander's death or Livy's report about Hannibal's vinegar-on-the-rocks. Orrery, himself, indulges in some trifling objections and moral reflections on what Swift presents and why he presents it. Book IV shows that Swift "has indulged a misanthropy that is intolerable" in giving human nature a representation that "must terrify, and even debase the mind of the reader who views it." Melancholy broods o'er Houyhnhnmland, Swift's wit and humor losing all their force. The reader is disgusted, not entertained; shocked, not instructed. "In painting Yahoos, Swift becomes one himself." The horses are cold, insipid, incapable of real virtue because they have neither motive nor power to act otherwise. Book IV is a "real insult upon mankind." — From *Remarks on the Life and Writings of Dr. Jonathan Swift* (London, 1752).

Patrick Delany

Delany frankly sets out to correct what he calls "various, evil, and ignorant accounts" abroad in the world about Dr. Swift. He admits Orrery's charges of Swift's "many filthy ideas and indecent expressions" throughout his work (a fault against what Delany calls "purity of style"); but he resents Orrery's supposing they came from his Irish associations. Swift's "defilement" he traces to Pope's bad influence. He agrees with Orrery in finding Swift's genius at fault for deriving so little "either of information or delight" from the account of the island of sorcerers and from the flying island (the latter might have developed into a noble illustration of the rule of divine Providence over the earth). Swift failed, Delany thinks, because his genius was "verging toward a decline." Swift had trifled away his genius on bagatelles and could not thereafter "rise to anything truly great or sublime." He had given away to sourness of temper and had increasingly indulged his passions. Stella's death had removed a sweetening influence, and passions became predominant over reason in him. He also wasted himself continually in excessive physical exercise. Delany implies that the *Travels* had some relationship to Swift's final "state of idiotism," with the voyage to the Houyhnhnms "a piece more deform, erroneous, and (of consequence) less instructive and agreeable, than any of his productions." His picture of the Yahoos "is too offensive to be copied ... debasing the human form to the lowest degree of a defiled imagination. Delany hopes that in the Yahoos Swift intended to satirize only human corruptions. In effect, he has constructed a panegyric on the human frame by suggesting the clumsiness of the noblest sub-human animal, the horse, in trying to do the things that human hands do very easily. Delany waxes clumsily satiric in suggesting the details of the absurdities Swift puts upon his horses; they could not be "serious to any other purpose than that of abandoned satire." Swift (Delany says it several times) in writing Book IV had taken leave of his own reason, and the satire fails because it enlarges human deformities beyond men's ability to recognize their own likeness in it. Man may be shocked, but he will not be amended.

Finally, Delany affirms his opinion that "if Swift had recovered one hour of rational reflection, after the signal chastisement of his total infatuation, he would have numbered his latter works among the follies of his life." But, in a postscript, Delany comments that Swift himself was entirely unlike the Yahoos, being in person "one of the cleanliest men that ever lived; cleanly in every character and circumstance of that personal virtue, to the utmost exactness, and even feminine nicety." Delany's critical remarks exhibit more of solid piety and moralism than they do of anything strictly literary. — From *Observations upon Lord Orrery's Remarks on the Life and Writings of Dr. Jonathan Swift* (London, 1754).

Samuel Johnson

Of Swift's style in his works other than *A Tale of a Tub*, Johnson judges that Swift found "an equable tenour of easy language, which rather trickles than flows. His delight was in simplicity . . . his few metaphors seem to be received rather by necessity than by choice. He studied purity . . . it is not often that solecism can be found; and whoever depends on his authority may generally conclude himself safe. His sentences are never too much dilated or contracted; and it will not be easy to find any embarrassment in the complication of his clauses, and inconsequence in his connections, or abruptness in his transitions. His style was well suited to his thoughts, which are never subtilized by nice disquisitions, decorated by sparkling conceits, elevated by ambitious sentences, or variegated by far-sought learning. He pays no court to the passions; he excites neither surprise nor admiration; he always understands himself; and his reader always understands him: the peruser of Swift wants little previous knowledge: it will be sufficient that he is acquainted with common words and common things; he is neither required to mount elevations, nor to explore profundities; his passage is always on a level, along solid ground, without asperities, without obstruction.

"This easy and safe conveyance of meaning it was Swift's desire to attain, and for having attained it he deserves praise, though perhaps not the highest praise." It is suitable for merely teaching what is previously unknown, but it makes no headway against the inattention that neglects truths already known.

Johnson is impressed with the "depravity of intellect" with which Swift delighted "in revolving ideas from which almost every other mind shrinks with disgust." What can allure the mind, Johnson wants to know, in "disease, deformity, and filth?" And he assures his reader that the mind that had described the Yahoos "had nothing filthy to learn." — From "Swift" in *Lives of the English Poets* (London, 1781).

Thomas Sheridan

Sheridan, more aggressively than Delany, writes to oppose the false picture of Swift given in Orrery's *Remarks*. But he is angrily severe (and very logical) with Samuel Johnson as well. To Sheridan, Swift was in many ways a man of eminent virtue who had been maligned by Orrery's scanty and erroneous "facts." He defends Swift against charges of ambition and avarice. Against the charge of misanthropy, chiefly founded on the "supposed satyr of human nature" in the Yahoos, Sheridan opposes the claim that the whole epilogue of the Houyhnhnms and Yahoos "is evidently designed to shew in what the true dignity and perfection of man's nature consists, and to point out the way by which it may be attained."

The last book, he says, gives "two new portraits; one, of pure unmixed vice; the other, of perfect unadulterated virtue" to raise abhorrence of the one and attraction for the other. The Yahoo, "a creature of fancy," bears "no resemblance to man, but in the make of its body, and the vicious propensities of its nature." It has no soul, no reason, and it goes upon all fours. Yahoos' long, hooked claws are not the nails of man merely extended. Even in body the Yahoo is beast, not man. On the other hand, the Houyhnhnms show collected "all the virtues, all the great qualities" which dignify man's nature," and the obvious inference to draw is that Swift intends a lesson to men "not to suffer the animal part to be predominant in them, lest they resemble the vile Yahoo, and fall into vice and misery, but to emulate the noble and generous Houyhnhnms, by cultivating the rational faculty to the utmost, which will lead them to a life of virtue and happiness."

Sheridan finds it extraordinary that men insist on finding their resemblance in the beast and not in the creature that has their distinguishing marks of reason and speech. Why are men so stupid as to stop at the outside of an avowed fable, when the moral of all fable is within? Sheridan also attacks commentators other than Orrery who have interpreted the *Travels* as misanthropic. Does it never occur to these people, as they take squeamish offense at Swift's non-entity, his chimera of the brain, that thousands of actual men are more detestable than the Yahoos (and he supplies examples both savage and civilized)? Sheridan treats Dr. Johnson's account of Swift with great and justified rigor for its carelessness about facts, for its obvious desire to condemn Swift (in Johnson's observations he finds "a striking instance of that leveling principle in mankind, which swallows with avidity any slanders propagated to the disadvantage of exalted characters." He proves Johnson an avowed enemy of Swift's who makes charges "not from his own knowledge, but from hearsay; and that too in the most guarded manner"). Johnson is so unjust and so inhumane as a biographer of Swift that his judgment on other writers also should be suspect. Savage, for example, who follows Swift in the *Lives of the English Poets*, receives twice the amount of attention from Johnson that the far superior Swift does. — From "The Life of Dr. Swift," in *The Works of Jonathan Swift* (17 vols.; London, 1784), vol. 1.

Sir Walter Scott

For Books I, II, and III Scott explains what he can of the satire and its objects. He has no difficulties about structure. But in Book IV he says an editor of Swift "must ever consider with pain" the product of that fierce indignation "long gnawing on [Swift's] heart." His experience of Ireland's degradation, his ill health, his social misery, his decayed life, his banishment to a country he disliked, etc., "drove him to loathe the very species by whom such iniquity was done and suffered." Though the picture of the Yahoos is "utterly odious," it serves the moral purpose of showing to what our species is degraded by "the wilful subservience of mental qualities to animal instincts" (as may be found in "the degraded ranks of every society, when brutalized by ignorance and gross vice"). Yet, nothing can justify "the nakedness" of Swift's "horrible outline of mankind degraded to a bestial state."

Book IV is also less *probable* than the other three: giants and pygmies the reader can accept, but not horses that sow and reap, milk cows, and deposit milk in vessels which they could not make. (Here Scott borrows from Delany.) Among writers of utopias, says Scott, Swift alone enlivened morality with humor, relieved absurdity with satire, and gave most improbable events a seeming reality by means of the character and style of their narrator. Gulliver is a very *real* and strictly English character. The observance of proportion in Books I and II lessens the effect of the marvelous (gives more verisimilitude). Scott admires many of the touches of art ("a thousand masterly touches of art") by which Swift converts an "extravagant fairy tale into a narrative, unequalled for the skill with which it is sustained, and the genuine spirit of satire of which it is made the vehicle." — From *Memoirs of Jonathan Swift* (2 vols.; Edinburgh, 1814).

William Hazlitt

Swift's style, along with that of Arbuthnot, Steele, and the other writers of Queen Anne's time, was English, as Dr. Samuel Johnson's was not. They looked about them for "the properest word to convey any idea." Hazlitt terms Johnson's ill-natured criticism of Swift "futile as well as invidious," and finds in the *Travels* "a power that has moved the world," and "the power is not that of big words and vaunting commonplaces." Swift's purpose, "to strip empty pride and grandeur of the imposing air which external circumstances throw around them," is achieved by "cheating the imagination" of its illusions produced by the "prejudices of sense and the world." In the end, it leaves nothing solid in mankind but wisdom and virtue. "What a libel is this upon mankind!"

exclaims Hazlitt, "What a convincing proof of misanthropy! What presumption and what *malice prepense*, to shew men what they are and to teach them what they ought to be!" What shocks Swift administers to national glory, to personal vanity! But Hazlitt cannot see harm, or misanthropy, or the "immoral and degrading tendency" in what Swift does. Nothing but imposture need complain of it. Hazlitt divorces himself from critics who cannot forget — at so long a distance — the political affiliations of Swift. He believes that Swift invented Brobdingnagians and Lilliputians to escape from the more painful realities of the world around him; for "*they* only made him laugh, while men and women made him angry." — From *Lectures on the English Poets*, Lecture VI, in *The Collected Works of William Hazlitt*, ed. A. R. Waller and Arnold Glover (London, 1902), vol. V.

William Makepeace Thackeray

Thackeray shows too much concern with the *personality* of Swift, which he represents as that of a bully and coward full of vanity, hypocrisy, servility to his superiors, arrogance, and bad manners; a social highwayman who failed to take the great prize he desired because the coach bearing it (a mitre and a crozier) never came where he waited to rob it. Thackeray mocks Swift with consistent sarcasm. Nothing Swift does or says, to Thackeray's mind, could possibly arise from a good motive. In *Gulliver*, he admires the "humor and conduct of this famous satire," but the moral he thinks "shameful, horrible, unmanly, blasphemous; and giant and great as this Dean is, I say we should hoot him." He advises his listeners not to read the last part of Gulliver, for the reader becomes, like Gulliver, "almost stifled with the filth" showered on him: "It is Yahoo language — a monster gibbering shrieks and gnashing imprecations against mankind; tearing down all shreds of modesty, past all sense of manliness and shame; filthy in word, filthy in thought, furious, raging, obscene."

In his "dreadful allegory," Swift intended to say that man "is utterly wicked, desperate and imbecile; and his passions are so monstrous and his boasted powers so mean that he is and deserves to be the slave of brutes, and ignorance is better than his vaunted reason. What had this man done? What secret remorse was rankling at his heart, what fever was boiling in him, that he should see all the world bloodshot?" Such feverish prejudice and misreading is not criticism. Swift as a humorist gets four paragraphs out of 41 pages (1893 edition) on Swift as one of Thackeray's *English Humorists*. — From "Swift," in *English Humorists of the Eighteenth Century* (London, 1893). The lecture was given in 1851.

Henry Craik

Craik quotes out of context the seriously misleading words of Swift

129

that his entire fabric was built upon the "foundation of misanthropy" and reveals his own tendency to *biographize* the *Travels* by saying "the book itself must be examined if we are to master an important chapter in the story of Swift's life." The book was written with Swift "face to face with approaching old age, with the fire of his consuming indignation burning more fiercely than before," unable to master his bitter hatred against mankind. In Book I, Swift "carefully maintains the circumstantiality" of the narrative. There is nothing unkindly in the laughter at mankind (here); only at the end of the book is there any revelation of vehement anger. Brobdingnag brings not less humor, but does bring more bitter and intense satire. Swift finds human nature "contemptible for its infinite pettiness and triviality, for its endless and futile restlessness: for its pigmy strainings to create difficulties." Brobdingnag does offer relief and amusement in the mishaps of Gulliver.

Book III begins (and Book IV continues) to show a failure in "the nicely adjusted proportions and the careful construction of the preceding voyages." The construction of the allegory fails, but the satire has increased directness. Book III is especially full of faults of construction, with the strokes being "constantly delivered, not with the impartiality of fable, but with the directness of personal spleen." Here, Swift reveals his melancholy, his views on the greatness of the past, the "morbid despair with which [he] awaited old age."

On the coarseness of Book IV, "we need not dwell." Its fable is clumsily constructed, its "comparison between the Houyhnhnms and their counterparts" often shows "mere verbal quibbling," the idea of horses ruling men lacks satiric force, and Swift deserts matters of general concern to attack special classes with which he was irritated. But the central contrast between Houyhnhnm and Yahoo leaves humanity "without a shred of defence for its own self-respect." The book passes from warning to despair; down go "the trappings and disguises with which we deceive ourselves;" and we are left "face to face with the stern realities of our nature and our lot." The book reveals Swift's scathing contempt of mankind. – From *The Life of Jonathan Swift* (London, 1882).

Leslie Stephen

Gulliver's Travels is not a book in which we take frank leave of the real world. Swift's fundamental assumptions we easily accept: Why should there not be creatures in which our feet represent inches or our inches feet? Instead of bewildering the imagination like Lucian and Rabelais, Swift agreeably stimulates it with "an extreme and exceptional case, but one to which all the ordinary laws of human nature are still strictly applicable." Yet Stephen finds the satire in its final development "congenial to the mental attitude of all who have persuaded themselves that men are, in fact, a set of contemptible fools and knaves, in whose quarrels and mutual slaughterings the wise and good could not persuade themselves to take a serious interest." If a man does not share Swift's sentiments, no mere change in the scale will convince him that he is right.

Swift, says Stephen, has provided "for the man who despises his species a number of exceedingly effective symbols for the utterance of his contempt" and "a whole gallery of caricatures thoroughly congenial to the despisers of humanity." Stephen dwells on what he calls "the most unpleasant part of Swift's character..., a morbid interest in the physically disgusting.... The objection to Swift is not that he spoke plainly, but that he brooded over filth unnecessarily." Swift's "indulgence in revolting images" he finds "to some extent an indication of a diseased condition of mind, perhaps of actual mental decay." By the Yahoos, Swift shows his belief that in man the bestial predominates. Meanwhile, the Houyhnhnms represent his utopia. But the satirist's view of the nature of man is "too black to admit of any hopes of their millennium." Stephen, however, does get round to seeing in Swift a real philanthropy underlying his misanthropy and a "righteous hatred of brutality and oppression which is but the seamy side of a generous sympathy." Stephen wants it both ways; he has not distinguished Gulliver from Swift. — From *Swift*, English Men of Letters Series (London, 1882; New York and London, 1902).

Charles Whibley

Swift is unusual in that his unhappy death did not free him from the rancors of critics who have treated him "not as a great historical figure, but as a miscreant who had inflicted upon them a personal injury" and from whom they sought vengeance instead of giving judgment. Thackeray has been especially violent and unjust, and the sinister figure of Swift he created had no reason to be in a gallery of humorists. Thackeray gave merely a Victorian prejudice, not a criticism. Swift cared nothing for a philanthropy that loved men in general and kicked them in particular. He loved his friends with a steady loyalty. Yet he had an eye for the "general infamy of men" and knew how rare a thing in the world an Arbuthnot was. Swift was a delightful and sought-after man, and he busied himself endlessly to promote his friends' welfare. No misanthrope, then, Swift was also no cynic. No heart torn with bitter indignation is a cynic's heart; Swift was a born idealist.

Critics have generally misread the meaning of *Gulliver's Travels*. Swift passes no "universal sentence upon the human race." (One might think of Captain Mendez or of the Brobdingnagian king.) Whibley finds it simply obvious that Swift's own creed is "the generous creed of the King of Brobdingnag." Two hundred years late we have discovered the truth of Swift's statement that "Whoever could make two ears of corn or two blades of grass to grow upon a spot of ground where only one grew before, would deserve better of mankind, and do more essential service to his country than the whole race of politicians put together." Only a "vain superstition of party can dismiss the moral of Gulliver as shameful, horrible, blasphemous." — From "Jonathan Swift," in *Literary Studies* (London, 1919).

Louis A. Landa

Landa insists on the need to separate the biography of Swift from critical thinking about *Gulliver's Travels*. Gulliver is not Swift, but a character in a satire on human institutions, foibles and vices. For well over two hundred years biographers and critics have selected isolated biographical facts to maintain a "horrendous image" of Swift as a misanthrope of "moral deformity" and "defiled imagination" whose purpose was to expose the human race as beastly, nasty, brutal, contemptible and utterly repulsive. Such writers have consistently called Book IV of the *Travels* an artistic failure because they found it morally culpable — not being able to separate artistry from morals in their critical operations. Nineteenth-century critics like Sir Walter Scott, Edmund Gosse, and W. E. H. Lecky tried to escape facing up to the problems of Book IV by saying that Swift's work here shows that he was "more or less mad," that he was writing under "incipient mental disease," or that his misanthropy sprang from a melancholy "mainly due to a physical malady which had long acted upon his brain." Twentieth-century psychoanalysts have translated this nineteenth-century attitude into psychological terms. But such reliance upon a theory of insanity, Landa points out, is weakened by 1) *ex post facto* reasoning (reasoning *after* the fact): Swift's mental powers failed towards the end of his life, 15 or 16 years *after* the appearance of the *Travels*; 2) Book III was written *after* Book IV, yet "insanity" is not found in Book III; 3) *The Drapier's Letters*, praised by these same commentators for the "vigor, the keenness, the sanity, and the humanity of the mind that produced" them, were written *after* Swift completed the draft of Book IV; 4) these and other critics of Swift tend to seize isolated, out-of-context statements and make them unduly important because such statements support what the critics want to prove. Landa cites as an example the *report* that late in life Swift bade his friends good-bye with "Good night, I hope I shall never see you again." "If," Landa challenges, "Swift really used this remark, if he used it seriously, some weight may be attached to it; but I should want to know to whom he used it and in what tone or spirit." Swift was famous for his teasing banter, his "manner of friendly insult;" his friends knew the affection behind his upside-down compliments, which, if taken literally, offer poor ground for either literary or psychological judgments. Swift was, until his last years, playful, witty, full of zest for life.

But, Landa holds, some biographical approaches important to

criticism of Swift have been neglected. Swift was a clergyman, and one who discharged his duties scrupulously. His sermons, like other eighteenth-century sermons, held no optimistic view of human nature. One of his sermons begins:

> The holy Scripture is full of expressions to set forth the miserable condition of man during the whole progress of his life; his weakness, pride, and vanity, his unmeasurable desires, and perpetual disappointments; the prevalency of his passions, and the corruptions of his reason, his deluding hopes, and his real, as well as imaginary, fears . . . his cares and anxieties, the diseases of his body, and the diseases of his mind. . . . And the wise men of all ages have made the same reflections.

This is precisely the material of *Gulliver's Travels*, and, Landa observes, "there is no need to ascribe such views solely to personal bitterness or frustrations or melancholia." Book IV reflects a standard Christian position of the eighteenth century. Swift had no sympathy with strong assertions of man's goodness or man's capacity for virtue. "Swift the clergyman repeats himself in *Gulliver's Travels*." — From *English Institute Essays, 1946* (New York, 1947).

Ricardo Quintana

Quintana thinks that a great many readers in 1726, when the *Travels* appeared, reacted as did Dr. Arbuthnot when he judged Gulliver "a happy man that at his age can write such a merry work." The statement shows the "kind of audience Swift was writing for." What formerly passed as Swift's pessimism now strikes us as common sense, and beside present-day satiric writings it may prove a cheerful book. We now understand the book better than it was formerly understood, are better prepared to perceive its artistry and craftsmanship, do not recoil from its positive doctrines, and are probably "readier to acknowledge that its meaning as an imaginative statement" is separable from its "merely logical or common sense meanings." But what has kept *Gulliver's Travels* alive is Swift's comic artistry. Whatever the political allegory or allegories included in the book, "*Gulliver's Travels* is a satiric comedy cast in the form of the imaginary voyage." As an eighteenth-century book it met the demands of its time. It pleased and it instructed. Its views of fallen man, of politics, and history reflect the views of Swift's time with their basis in Christian and classical traditionalism. In all the four voyages, society as a matter of course is organized according to classes (as it was in Swift's England). Nobles are not confused with servants, nor does Swift suggest upsetting the arrangement. Government ideally is balanced, with no tyranny of prince or nobles or commons. Gulliver is no primitivist. If, Quintana observes, Gulliver ultimately turns upon everything at home, it is not because Europe is too civilized but because Europe is degenerating from true civilization.

Even in his madness Gulliver never ceases to be part of a comedy. The letter from Captain Gulliver — added in 1735 but pretending to date from six months after the first publication — enforced the comic view of the various evils Gulliver has attacked. It amusingly summarizes what the indignant Gulliver has not found to happen. He had desired of his cousin that

> . . . you would let me know by a Letter . . . a thousand other
> Reformations, I firmly counted upon . . . as indeed they were
> plainly deducible from the Precepts delivered in my Book.

Quintana suggests three structural patterns running through the book and maintaining a comic situation: the actual travel book, the imaginary travel book, and the parody of the imaginary travel book. By overdoing all utopias this last pattern laughs at utopia-making itself. Thus, the care in Lilliput to avoid spoiling children becomes by its excessiveness a leg-pulling of the utopian imaginary voyages:

> Their Parents are suffered to see them only twice a Year; the
> Visit is not to last above an Hour; they are allowed to kiss the
> Child at Meeting and Parting; but a Professor, who always
> standeth by on those Occasions, will not suffer them to
> whisper, or use any fondling Expressions, or bring any
> Presents of Toys, Sweet-meats, and the like.

Quintana tries to justify the break between Books II and IV as illogical but artistic. "Part IV begins, psychologically, where the second leaves off, for the intensity of Gulliver's reactions produces in him a state of shock which causes him to lose his self-esteem as one of the human race." The intervention of Book III, "scattered in its effects and only once — in the episode of the struldbrugs — producing a marked psychic reaction on Gulliver's part, is almost a functional necessity." It breaks tension like the scherzo in a four-movement symphony.

His rejection as "little vermin" by the Brobdingnagian king drives Gulliver into a self-defensive pride in which he convinces himself that the estimable characteristics of the Brobdingnagians are absurd and that Europe has virtues it does not.

Quintana speaks of ironic refraction through the distorting medium of a character as a structural quality of *Gulliver's Travels* to present Swift's ideas. To distinguish what is public statement from what is direct in what a character says, and to know just where dramatic presentation begins "is sometimes a nice [question] for the reader." The "extraordinary effects" of Swift's masterpiece of comic art arise from the "ironic refraction supplied by Gulliver." The comedy depends, as well, upon exclusion, especially in Books II and IV. In Book I, normal, English Gulliver, unacquainted with being an outsider, does not suffer from his exclusion from Lilliputian society, for he has rejected that puny society. In Brobdingnag, however, he is stung by his exclusion as one of "a race of little odious vermin," and he suffers a retraction of himself into the defensive pride noticed previously. Book III brings no such crisis; but Book IV, from Chapter 2 to the end, presents Gulliver as an "unwholesome deviate." The pattern of "ironic refraction and the comedy of exclusion" is the principle of composition in the climactic voyage to the Houyhnhnms. — From *Swift, An Introduction* (London, New York, Toronto, 1955).

Herbert Davis

Gulliver's Travels is wholly of the eighteenth century. It shares the typical interest of Swift's time in history as a comment on human behavior. It uses, like other commentaries on history, the weapon of satire. But its explorations are conducted in imaginary realms rather than in the nations of actual history. In part, the book disguises the history of the times of Queen Anne which Swift desired to write. Using the travel-book form enabled Swift to employ the satirical methods he had long since perfected (parody, raillery, irony) and to make a masterpiece that united the experience of his London political career and that of his own life.

Though we can, with Gulliver, view Lilliput most of the time with an amused detachment, in Books II and IV Swift found a better means of keeping his imaginary world in proper balance with the real one and of making most profitable use of all his own experience. But in Book III the confusion and lack of unity are due partly to his use of material he himself has never really assimilated (Royal Society experiments, the "extravagancies of the virtuosos"). Readers have felt Book III confused and less effective than Books I, II, and IV because after the book was finished Swift was attempting to add new material that would celebrate his own recent triumph in Ireland (over Wood's coinage) and would use the materials he had, with Dr. Arbuthnot, collected in early 1726 about experiments then actually being conducted.

The real greatness of the *Travels* is in its being "the final and completest satire on human life of this Christian moralist," and it is this character of the book that has disturbed readers who label Swift mad, monstrous, blasphemous, abnormal, inhumanly cold and disloyal, and not to be trusted. He disliked the way of the world and he set down his testimony against it. Swift's "peculiar satisfaction" was to use all his skills and "all the tricks of his trades" to "make us see what a world we live in, to make us feel its brutality" and degradation, to upset our complacencies, and to "leave us unreconciled to the 'unestimable sum of human pain.' " — From *Jonathan Swift, Essays on his Satire and Other Studies* (New York, 1964).

Bibliography

Barroll, J. Leeds. "Gulliver and the Struldbrugs," *Publications of the Modern Language Association* LXXIII (1958), 43-50.

Brady, Frank, ed., *Twentieth Century Interpretations of Gulliver's Travels*, Englewood Cliffs, N.J., 1968.

————— , "Vexations and Diversions: Three Problems in *Gulliver's Travels*," *Modern Philology* LXXV (1978), 346-67.

Bullitt, John M. *Jonathan Swift and the Anatomy of Satire*. Cambridge, Mass., 1953.

Case, Arthur. *Four Essays on Gulliver's Travels*. Gloucester, Mass., 1958.

Carnochan, W. B. *Lemuel Gulliver's Mirror for Man*. Berkeley, 1968.

Clark, Paul O. *A Gulliver Dictionary*, Chapel Hill, 1953.

Clubb, Merrel D. "The Criticism of Gulliver's 'Vogage to the Houyhnhnms,' 1726-1914," *Stanford Studies in Language and Literature* (1941), 203-232.

Downie, J. A. "Political Characterization in *Gulliver's Travels* " *Yearbook of English Studies* VII (1977), 108-120.

Eddy, William A. *Gulliver's Travels: A Critical Study*. Gloucester, Mass., 1963.

Ehrenpreis, Irvin. *The Personality of Swift*. London, 1958.

—————. *Mr. Swift and his Contemporaries*. London, 1962.

—————. "The Meaning of Gulliver's Last Voyage," *Review of English Literature* III (1962), 18-38.

Elliott, Robert C. "Gulliver as Literary Artist," *Journal of English Literary History* XIX (1952), 49-63.

—————. The Power of Satire. Princeton, 1960.

—————. "Swift's Satire: Rules of the Game" *Journal of English Literary History* XXXXI (1974), 413-428.

Ewald, William B. *The Masks of Jonathan Swift*. Cambridge, 1954.

Foster, Milton, ed. *A Casebook on Gulliver among the Houyhnhnms*. N.Y., 1961.

Gravil, Richard, ed. *Swift-Gulliver's Travels: A Casebook*. London, 1974.

Greenberg, Robert A., ed. *Gulliver's Travels: An Annotated Text with Critical Essays*, N.Y., 1961.

Hunting, Robert. *Jonathan Swift*, N.Y., 1967.

Kliger, Samuel. "The Unity of *Gulliver's Travels*," *Modern Language Quarterly*, VI (1945), 405-415.

Landa, Louis A. and J. E. Tobin. *Jonathan Swift: A List of Critical Studies Published from 1895 to 1945*, N.Y., 1945.

Leavis, F. R. "The Irony of Swift," *Scrutiny*, (March 1934), 364-78.

Moore, John B. "The Role of Gulliver," *Modern Philology*, XXV (1928), 469-480.

Morrissey, L. J. *Gulliver's Progress*. Hamden, Conn., 1978.

Nicolson, Marjorie. *Science and Imagination*. Ithaca, N.Y., 1956. (see esp. 110-154).

Orwell, George. "Politics vs. Literature: An Examination of *Gulliver's Travels*," in *Shooting an Elephant and Other Essays*. N.Y., 1950.

Pinkus, Philip. *Swift's Vision of Evil: A Comparative Study of a Tale of a Tub and Gulliver's Travels*. Victoria, B.C., 1975. (Vol. II — *Gulliver's Travels*.)

Potter, George R. "Swift and Natural Science," *Philological Quarterly* (January, 1941), 97-118.

Price, Martin. *Swift's Rhetorical Art: A Study in Structure and Meaning*, New Haven, 1953.

Quintana, Ricardo. *Two Augustans: John Locke, Jonathan Swift*. Madison, Wisc., 1978.

_____. *The Mind and Art of Jonathan Swift*, London, 1953.

_____. *Swift: An Introduction*, London, 1955.

Rawson, Claude, ed. *Focus: Swift*, London, 1971.

Rogers, Pat. "Gulliver and the Engineers," *Modern Language Review* LXX (1975), 260-270.

Ross, John F. "The Final Comedy of Lemuel Gulliver," in *Studies in the Comic, University of California Publications in English*, VIII : 2 (1941), 175-196.

Rowse, A. L. *Jonathan Swift*. N.Y., 1976.

Stathis, James J. *A Bibliography of Swift Studies, 1945-1965*, Nashville, Tenn., 1967.

Stone, Edward. "Swift and the Horses: Misanthropy or Comedy?" *Modern Language Quarterly* X (1949), 367-376.

Sutherland, John N. "A Reconsideration of Gulliver's Third Voyage," *Studies in Philology* LIV (January, 1957), 45-52.

Tilton, John W. "*Gulliver's Travels* as a Work of Art," *Bucknell Review* VIII (December, 1959), 246-259.

Traugott, John. "A Voyage to Nowhere with Thomas More and Jonathan Swift . . .," *Sewanee Review* LXIX (Autumn, 1961), 534-565.

_____, ed. *Discussions of Jonathan Swift*, Boston, 1962.

Tuveson, Ernest. "Swift: The Dean as Satirist," *University of Toronto Quarterly* XXII (1953), 368-375.

_____, ed. *Swift: A Collection of Critical Essays*, New Jersey, 1964.

Voight, Milton. *Swift and the Twentieth Century*, Detroit, 1964.

Ward, David. *Jonathan Swift: An Introductory Essay*. London, 1973.

Wedel, T. O. "On the Philosophical Background of *Gulliver's Travels*," *Studies in Philology* XXIII (October, 1926), 434-450.

Williams, Kathleen. "Gulliver's Voyage to the Houyhnhnms," *A Journal of English Literary History* XVIII (1951), 275-286.

————. "Animal Rationis Capax...," *A Journal of English Literary History* XXI (1954), 193-207.

————. *Jonathan Swift and the Age of Compromise*, Lawrence, Kansas, 1958.

————. *Swift: The Critical Heritage*, London, 1970.